Urge

A Comedy

John Scholes

Samuel French – London
New York – Sydney – Toronto – Hollywood

ESSEX COUNTY LIBRARY

ISBN 0 573 11478 1

EV79984

CHARACTERS

Malcolm Stevenson
Adele Dumbrovski
Mildred Fogerty
Daphne Delgrado
Pierre Dubois
Monica Delgrado
Detective Sergeant Walter Tomkins
Detective Sergeant John Holmes
Gloria Lane

The action takes place in a lighthouse two miles off the English coast

ACT I   Evening
ACT II   Seconds later

Time—1944

ACT I

A lighthouse on an island two miles off the English coast. 1944, evening

The main area is the room at the base of the lighthouse. This is haphazardly furnished with large crates with lids UR *and* UL, *tea-chests and boxes. A small radio sits on one box. Lengths of string and wire are festooned around the room, with bits of debris hanging from them; ship's lanterns, lifebelts, shells etc. An image of peculiarity and eccentricity pervades.* L *is a door which leads outside. Another door* R *leads to the kitchen, bedrooms etc., and a third door upstage opens on to stairs leading to the top part of the lighthouse.* UR *is the top part of the lighthouse itself, which is raised from the main acting area. In the top part is a practical window and a makeshift camp bed. There are a number of books scattered around*

When the CURTAIN *rises the bed in the top part of the lighthouse is occupied by Malcolm Stevenson, but only his bare feet can be seen poking from under the blanket*

Adele Dumbrovski enters L. *She is in her thirties, American and attractive. She wears a swimsuit and is wet. She peers cautiously round the room*

Adele (*calling*) Anyone at home? (*She crosses to the door* R, *opens it and calls through it*) Anybody there? For Pete's sake somebody's got to be somewhere. Mr Fogerty! Are you there? Mrs Fogerty! (*She closes the door; looking around in disgust*) Heavens to Murgatroyd! What a way to run a war. (*She tries to open the upstage door. It is locked*) Hey! Can anybody hear me?

There is no response

Somebody better come soon. (*Calling out*) This is a life and death job. D'you hear me? If nobody makes their presence felt soon it will be the end of civilization as we know it. (*Looking around the room; to herself*) Although it looks as though civilization hasn't reached this neck of the woods yet. (*She sits on a packing case and shivers; to herself*) What the hell. Why should I care? I've only swum two miles of ocean to save the British Empire from a fate worse than castration and nobody wants to know. Typical. Absolutely typical. (*Standing and shouting*) Listen, you Limeys. How would you like a Jerry under every bed? 'Cos that's what will happen if I don't get some sort of co-operation situation going soon. (*She waits for a response. There is none*) Mr Fogerty! Anybody! (*After a pause*) OK, Winston Churchill will have to fight them on the beaches himself. Hope he's got some pretty strong cigars. Haysus Christus!

Adele exits L

There is a short pause

Mildred Fogerty enters upstage. She is in her sixties, vague, deaf and happy. She wears a tatty dressing-gown and carries a bundle of clothing. She sings the first few lines of "I'm In The Mood For Love" to herself sexily. She twiddles the radio knob but nothing comes out

Mildred Damn it. They don't make wirelesses like they used to. I blame that Ramsey MacDonald. Him and that Kaiser Bill. Everything's rubbish these days. Nothing but rubbish. (*She picks up the radio and shakes it*) I'm missing Gracie Fields again. There's no justice. No justice at all. The world's gone to pot. (*She replaces the radio*)

Mildred exits R

Malcolm Stevenson stirs on the bed in the top part of the lighthouse. His feet twitch and he sits up. He is in his twenties and good looking. He yawns and looks weary. He gets out of bed. He wears underpants. He looks around for his clothes. He can't find them

Stevenson Bleeding hell. Where's my gear? (*He sits on the bed and ponders*) Bloody wash day again. Every day's wash day. Monday's wash day. Tuesday's wash day. Wens-bloody-day is wash day. (*Calling out in anguish*) Can't I have one day that isn't wash day? Can't I just have a pair of socks that are a bit grubby? Do I always have to be pristine clean? I mean, I can't go very far on an island two miles by one, can I? Who do I have to impress, eh? The seagulls? (*In disgust he returns to his bed and pulls the covers over him*)

Mildred enters R, *carrying two glasses of lemonade*

Mildred (*singing to herself*) "Love walked right in, de dum de dum de de dum . . ."

She exits through the upstage door

Adele enters L

Adele (*calling*) Mr Fogerty! I know you're here somewhere. Please, Mr Fogerty, I'm not in the mood for games right now. You're old enough to know better. If I find you do I get a prize? A conducted tour around the lighthouse maybe? An autographed photo of Lassie? Aw c'mon, Mr Fogerty, this is pretty silly, you know that? I'm here to save all our lives and all you can do is make like the invisible man. Not real smart, Mr Fogerty.

She exits L

Mildred enters the top part of the lighthouse

Mildred (*to Stevenson*) Refreshments.
Stevenson (*sitting up*) Where are my clothes?
Mildred Your favourite, lemonade.

Stevenson (*shouting*) I said where are my clothes? And I hate lemonade.

Mildred I knew you'd be pleased.

Stevenson Are you plugged in?

Mildred And I've got carrot cake later.

Stevenson I said are you plugged in? Can you hear me?

Mildred You'll have to speak up, I can't hear you.

Stevenson I said—oh, never mind.

Mildred hands Stevenson the lemonade

Mildred Radio's on the blink again.

Stevenson Oh?

Mildred So's my hearing aid.

Stevenson Pity.

Mildred No need to be crude.

Stevenson I said—oh, never mind.

Mildred I think it's the BBC's fault.

Stevenson (*wearily*) What is?

Mildred My hearing aid going on the blink. It's all those funny air waves and stuff.

Stevenson What funny air waves?

Mildred The ones they keep putting out. You know, to confuse the enemy.

Stevenson The Germans aren't so confused as I am.

Mildred What?

Stevenson I said—oh, never mind.

Mildred Everybody sounds like Donald Duck. I blame Chamberlain. He's not hard of hearing so he doesn't care.

Stevenson Look, Mildred, why don't you go and make your carrot cake?

Mildred It's made.

Stevenson Then let's have a Bombay duck.

Mildred No need to be crude.

Stevenson And could I please have some clothes? I know you'd like to keep me stuck at the top of the lighthouse forever but——

Mildred Are you complaining?

Stevenson (*quickly*) No—no. I'm not complaining.

Mildred I should hope not.

Stevenson Mrs Fogerty——

Mildred (*admonishing*) Now, now. Mildred.

Stevenson Mildred, I shall always be utterly, eternally grateful for what you've done for me but I think——

Mildred You think far too much. That's the problem with today's young people.

Stevenson (*worked up*) Will you let me finish a sentence?

Mildred You're a long way from finishing *your* sentence.

Stevenson (*sighing*) All right. Point taken.

Mildred I don't know why you're complaining.

Stevenson I'm not complaining. It's just that——

Mildred You've got a nice little place here.

Stevenson I know, but I'd like to——

Mildred Away from those nasty guns and things that go bang, crash boom.

Stevenson I know, but I'd like to——

Mildred And I won't tell anybody that you're here.

Stevenson I know. I trust you, but——

Mildred Of course, if you'd rather be fighting over in France somewhere rather than here with little Mildred I could always tell the authorities where you are and then——

Stevenson You wouldn't—would you, Mildred?

Mildred (*patting his hand*) Course not, Malcolm. You like it here, don't you?

Stevenson It's paradise.

Mildred Don't worry. No nasty little sergeant's going to take my little Malcolm off to the war. You might get something shot off.

Stevenson That would be my luck.

Mildred No need to be crude.

Stevenson I said—oh, never mind.

Mildred You just stay here and read Alfred's books.

Stevenson But they're all in French.

Mildred I know.

Stevenson I don't understand French.

Mildred Alfred had this fixed idea that anything in French must be saucy.

Stevenson Well, they probably *are* saucy but they're written in French.

Mildred You're always complaining.

Stevenson Look, French was never my best subject at school. I never got beyond *arriverderci, mamma mia.*

Mildred Isn't that Spanish?

Stevenson There you are, I didn't get as far as I thought.

Mildred (*smiling and ruffling his hair*) You're a tease, Malcolm. I'm so glad you came here and not into the army.

Stevenson (*picking up a book*) Did Alfred ever figure out any of these books?

Mildred Well, I think he found the word "nude" in one of them once and it did seem to drive him ecstatic for a while.

Stevenson (*throwing down the book*) Bloody great.

Mildred But then, Alfred always was hot-blooded.

Stevenson Poor old Alfie.

Mildred He's happier than any of us.

Stevenson As long as they all don't speak French the other side of the pearly gates.

Mildred I don't think you should speak ill of the departed, Malcolm.

Stevenson I bet he never had to get around with no clothes all the time.

Mildred He always looked like he had clothes on when he had no clothes on.

Stevenson Can I have mine soon, please?

Mildred They're being washed.

Stevenson I know. They're always being washed.

Mildred You don't need them.

Stevenson Once in a while I'd like to get away from this tower and look around the island. See birds and flowers and smell the sea breeze.

Mildred But you might be seen.

Stevenson (*shouting*) Who's going to see me? A few seals? A couple of cormorants?

Mildred The recruiting people have eyes everywhere.

Stevenson You just like to see me without my clothes on, don't you?

Mildred (*offended*) Why, Malcolm, what are you implying?

Stevenson Nothing. I just hope this bloody war is over soon.

Mildred But you are playing an important part in the war, Malcolm my sweet. You keep this lighthouse going.

Stevenson And when they find out it's me and not Alfred Fogerty then it's goodbye freedom, hello justice.

Mildred You young people are all so pessimistic. I must look at my carrot cake. (*She motions towards the kitchen*)

Stevenson (*picking up a book*) Have a look at this book with me.

Mildred sits on the bed beside Stevenson

Any idea what *Chaussons à la Cussy* means?

Daphne Delgrado enters L, *into the main area of the lighthouse. She is fortyish, well dressed and neurotic. She is accompanied by Pierre Dubois, a dapper Frenchman; urbane and self assured*

Daphne (*to Pierre*) They must not have heard our motor launch come in. There's no greeting.

Pierre You expected maybe zee big hug and sloppy kisses after all zees years?

Daphne (*coldly*) Don't be terribly superior, Pierre. I may have had little to do with my mother and father in the last few years but I am still their daughter.

Pierre And because of this they should put up the tricoleur for you and sing the *Marseillaise*?

Daphne (*icily*) Pierre, at times you can be so . . . so . . .

Pierre So French?

Daphne So obnoxious.

Pierre Sorry, ma petite.

Daphne Sorry is not enough.

Pierre (*with exaggerated charm*) Oh, shall I prostrate my unworthy body before you and beg you to be merciful on such a humble person as myself? (*He throws himself on the floor*)

Daphne (*embarrassed*) Pierre, get up. Don't be so . . . so . . .

Pierre (*looking up*) So French?

Daphne So ridiculous. Honestly, as if I didn't have enough problems already with Monica without you playing the court jester.

Pierre But, mon amour, you know I would do anything for you. Anything.

Daphne Well, the first thing you can do for me is get up and stop behaving so . . . so . . .

Pierre So disgracefully?

Daphne So French.

Pierre (*rising*) Oui, ma sweet.

Daphne Where's Monica?

Pierre She was with us when we left the boat.

Daphne I know that, lame-brain, but she isn't with us now.

Pierre She is probably picking the daisies.

Daphne She has no right to pick daisies. She shouldn't be out of my sight.

Pierre She will be all right.

Daphne All right? It's all very well for you. She's not your daughter. I have
the worries of a mother, a caring, fond mother. Anything could happen to
her.

Pierre Believe me, my dear Daphne, very little can happen to her on a
barren island in the middle of nowhere.

Daphne She could be ravished. Raped. Indecently propositioned.

Pierre Who by? A grey seal?

Daphne You can act that way, but I'm her mother, her caring——

Pierre I know, I know, her loving mother who would rather see her dead
than in the arms of a sex-crazed grey seal.

Daphne (*affecting tears*) Sometimes, Pierre, I think you don't care at all for
me.

Pierre (*putting his arms around her*) Oh come now, my little ball of woolly
fluff, you know you are the moon and the stars to me.

Daphne (*unsurely*) Well . . .

Pierre You are the sun, the earth, the very life itself.

Daphne (*wilting*) Well . . .

Pierre You mean more to me than the universe, the milky way, the——

Daphne Pierre—you wouldn't lie to me, would you?

Pierre (*offended*) Me? Lie to you? You are the most precious gem in the
whole treasure house of the world.

Daphne I know that. But would you lie to me?

Pierre (*innocently*) Why should I do such a thing, my little passion flower?

Daphne You haven't got the lusts after Monica, have you?

Pierre (*surprised*) Me? Monica? Mon Dieu, the very thought.

Daphne She's only a young schoolgirl.

Pierre I know this.

Daphne She's so innocent and sweet. She must be protected.

Pierre From terrible, desperate fiends such as myself?

Daphne No, I think I trust you.

Pierre Oh, thanks a bundle, baby.

Daphne But I don't trust Monica.

Pierre I think Monica is safer here than anywhere. After all, that was the
whole idea, was it not?

Daphne I just wish she wouldn't go wandering off.

Mildred rises from the bed in the top part of the lighthouse

Pierre (*resignedly*) Would you like me to go and find her?

Daphne Please, Pierre. She's such a young, innocent thing. I'd be so distraught if anything terrible happened to her. After all, I am her mother.

Pierre (*sighing*) I know . . . so you keep telling me.

Mildred exits from the top part of the lighthouse

Daphne (*upset*) Go on, mock me. Mock motherhood, mock maternal concern. You don't care. You're not her father. You only lust after her.

Pierre (*putting his arms around Daphne*) Please believe me, I do not lust after your daughter. It is only you I lust after.

Daphne (*outraged*) So that's it? You don't love me. You only lust after me. I knew it. My body, that's all you want. Any body. Even a young, sweet, innocent body. They're all the same to you hot-blooded French types.

Pierre (*confused*) I do *not* lust after your body.

Daphne That's because you don't love me. You men are all the same.

Pierre Believe me, darling, I love you.

Daphne And Monica?

Pierre I don't love her at all.

Daphne (*more upset*) Oh dear, and I wanted you to get on with her so much. It meant a lot to me that you and she got on well together.

Pierre But we do. We get on incredibly well together.

Daphne (*aggressively*) So you *are* lusting after her.

Pierre (*defensively*) No . . . no. I just love her.

Daphne (*threateningly*) You love her?

Pierre (*retreating*) No . . . no. I just lust after her. I mean . . .

Daphne (*advancing on him*) That poor, young innocent child. You'd take advantage, you'd force yourself, you'd——

Pierre I think I'll go and look for her.

Daphne (*adamantly*) You'll go nowhere near her, you Lothario, you.

Pierre But I thought——

Daphne Don't go near her. Don't touch her. I knew I shouldn't trust any man. She's just a young, innocent schoolgirl, do you hear?

Pierre Of course, mon amour, of course.

Daphne She has to be protected from sex-crazed men like you.

Pierre I agree.

Daphne Oh, how demanding it is to be a mother.

Mildred enters the main area by the upstage door, locking it behind her

Pierre (*to Daphne*) How formidable it must be.

Daphne You're not a mother. You wouldn't know.

Pierre True. I have never been a mother.

Mildred (*to Daphne*) Annabelle!

Daphne (*going to Mildred*) Hello, Mother. No I'm not Annabelle. I'm Daphne. Your second daughter. Remember?

Mildred Daphne.

Daphne That's right, Mother.

Mildred Daphne.

Daphne You've got it. Daphne. It's been a long time.

Mildred A long time.

Daphne That's right. How are you keeping?
Mildred Daphne.
Daphne Yes, Mother, Daphne. (*Aside to Pierre, touching her head*) I told you she was a little . . . you know.
Pierre (*to Mildred*) Enchanted to meet you, Mrs Fogerty.
Mildred (*curtsying*) Enchanted to meet you, Luigi.
Daphne No, Mother. This is not Luigi.
Mildred Not Luigi?
Daphne Not Luigi.
Mildred But you married Luigi.
Daphne That's all over.
Mildred All over?
Daphne All over.
Mildred Does he know that?
Daphne I think so.
Mildred (*holding out her hand to Pierre*) Enchanted to meet you, Mr——er . . .
Pierre Dubois.

Mildred simpers as Pierre holds her hand

Mildred Oh, I say, Mr——er . . .
Pierre Dubois.
Mildred (*sexy bit*) I must say it's lovely to meet you.
Pierre Likewise, madame.
Mildred Please call me Mildred.
Pierre (*kissing her hand*) Mildred. Enchanté.
Mildred (*thrilled*) Likewise, I'm sure, Monsieur whatsit.
Pierre Dubois.
Daphne (*slapping Pierre's hand*) Weren't you going to look for Monica?
Mildred Who's Monica?
Daphne Your granddaughter.
Mildred Oh? Where is the dear little thing?
Daphne Who knows? She could be picking daisies or being assaulted on the rocks.
Pierre (*to Mildred*) Daphne has a very vivid imagination.
Mildred She always has had, Mr—— whatsit . . .
Pierre Dubois.
Mildred (*gazing into Pierre's eyes*) I say, is this a fleeting visit or . . . do you intend to stay a while?
Daphne Well, Mother, there is a reason for our visit.
Mildred I thought there must be.
Daphne Where's Father?
Mildred Who?
Daphne Father.
Mildred Father? Father who?
Daphne Don't play games, Mother. My father. Where is he?
Mildred Ah . . . Well . . . Your father isn't what he was.
Daphne What is he now? A turnip?

Mildred (*taking Pierre's hand*) Daphne always did have a wonderful sense of humour.

Pierre Which I am sure she inherited from you, Mildred.

Mildred (*coquettishly*) Yes, well . . . I've had my moments, Mr——

Pierre Dubois.

Daphne Mother. Where *is* Father?

Mildred (*confused*) Well, Annabelle, I've told you——

Daphne (*exasperated*) Mother, I am Daphne, this is Pierre and I would like to know where Father is.

Mildred He's gone fishing.

Daphne Fishing?

Mildred That's right. How'd you guess?

Daphne But he hates fishing

Mildred Not any more.

Daphne When will he be back?

Mildred How long are you staying?

Daphne About two days.

Mildred He'll be three days.

Pierre Oh quelle shame. I was so looking forward to seeing him.

Mildred I'm sure he would have liked to have met you too, Mr—— er . . .

Pierre Dubois

Daphne Mother, you might as well know the truth. Luigi and I didn't work out. We've parted.

Mildred Just as well. You should never have married a Russian in the first place.

Daphne He was Italian. Mother, listen. I want to get Monica away from things. She gets all sorts of—well, ideas.

Mildred Monica who?

Daphne Monica Delgrado. Your granddaughter. She's boy mad. She needs to be away from it all. That's why I've brought her here.

Mildred Where is she?

Daphne I don't know. She's on the island somewhere. I just hope she hasn't been deflowered among the daisies. Oh dear, I'd better find her. Poor little Monica.

Daphne exits L

Mildred (*eyeing Pierre*) Poor old Annabelle. She was always slightly dotty, you know.

Pierre Where is Mr Fogerty?

Mildred Alfred? You don't really want to meet him.

Pierre Believe me, I would be most honoured to meet him.

Mildred You wouldn't like him.

Pierre What makes you say that?

Mildred Well . . . he smells.

Pierre So does garlic, but I love garlic.

Mildred Well . . . he's ignorant.

Pierre So are monkeys, but I love monkeys.

Mildred He's . . . Well, he gets . . . an urge.

Pierre (*suddenly interested*) Did you say URGE?

Mildred That's right.

Pierre Please tell me more about this URGE.

Mildred I don't think I should. It's disgusting.

Pierre No, no. You should not think this.

Mildred It's all very well you saying that. But I've had to live with it.

Pierre But the URGE is a good thing.

Mildred Not the way Alfie's got it.

Pierre I would so much like to meet your Alfie.

Mildred Why?

Pierre Because I too am with the URGE.

Mildred You?

Pierre Yes. The Universal Reunification of the German Empire. URGE.

Mildred But you're Italian.

Pierre No. I am French.

Mildred Aren't you on our side?

Pierre I am Vichy.

Mildred Alfred used to get like that sometimes.

Pierre (*urgently*) Please, Madame Fogerty, you must trust me.

Mildred (*coyly*) I wouldn't trust a Frenchman as far as I could throw one of your letters.

Pierre Please, madame, this is serious.

Mildred Do you like carrot cake?

Pierre Please, Mildred, I am here on a mission.

Mildred I make nice carrot cake.

Pierre My mission is to contact your husband——

Mildred Alfred never used to like my carrot cake.

Pierre He is one of us. A confederate.

Mildred He always said it tasted too much like carrots.

Pierre Mildred, I *must* meet Mr Fogerty.

Mildred You wouldn't like him.

Pierre Please . . . let's not go into that again.

Mildred He snores.

Pierre But he is an ally of my country, of Vichy. And he will help us win the war.

Mildred He molests women.

Pierre Please, Mrs Fogerty, I don't care if he interferes with male parrots, I must see him.

Mildred We haven't got a parrot.

Pierre That is so sad, I'll get you one.

Mildred Would you?

Pierre Yes. Now, where do I find your husband?

Mildred I think I prefer a cockatoo.

Pierre I'll get you one.

Mildred It should have a mate.

Pierre I'll get you two.

Mildred Will you?

Pierre Yes. Now I must speak with your husband.

Mildred Why?

Pierre (*trying to remain calm*) Because he will help us win the war.

Mildred I thought we'd won it.

Pierre It is still in progress.

Mildred You mean the Kaiser is still at it?

Pierre (*patiently*) That was World War I.

Mildred Well, I think they should have left well enough alone.

Pierre (*taking Mildred's hand*) Mildred, my country—France—is on the wrong side. They have all been deluded. Everyone in Britain has also been deluded. It is Churchill's fault.

Mildred Really?

Pierre Yes. Completely deluded. Now, ma cherie, where do I find Monsieur Fogerty?

Mildred Well, you could try the other side of the island. In Shipwreck Bay.

Pierre Thank you.

Mildred (*smiling*) Don't be too long. I'll be waiting for you. (*She goes to the door* R *singing*) "Darling, je vous aime beaucoup, je ne sais pas what to do, vous avez . . ."

Mildred exits R

Pierre shakes his head in bewilderment. He tries to open the upstage door to the top part of the lighthouse but it is locked. He exits L

In the top part of the lighthouse Stevenson throws a book down in disgust and gets out of bed. He does exercises

Unseen by him, Monica Delgrado appears at the window. She watches him, amused and impressed. Suddenly Stevenson sees her and does a double take. He grabs a blanket to cover himself

Stevenson (*finding his voice*) How'd you get up here?

Monica Do you think you could let me in?

Stevenson Oh . . . sure. (*He opens the window*)

Monica climbs in. She has an extremely well proportioned figure which is accentuated by her skimpy school uniform. She also wears a school hat. She is all of twenty years old. Stevenson cannot disguise his appreciation of her, as his eyes take in her charms. As she climbs in, she stumbles and he grabs her instinctively to support her, letting go of his blanket

Monica (*smiling sweetly*) Thanks, Grandad.

Stevenson Grandad?

Monica You *are* Grandad Fogerty, aren't you?

Stevenson Do I look like him?

Monica I've never met him. But you're not how I imagined him to be. Anyway, I'm Monica.

Stevenson (*picking up the blanket and wrapping it around himself*) I'm very pleased to meet you, Monica. But how did you get up here? It must be all of fifty feet high.

Monica I climbed up the lightning conductor.

Stevenson (*amazed*) Well I'll be blowed. I never thought of that. You must be very athletic.

Monica I was top gymnast at Burnley High.

Stevenson Was?

Monica I left school years ago.

Stevenson (*indicating her attire*) Then why the masquerade?

Monica (*fed up*) It's Mum. She wants to keep me ten years old. (*She sits on the bed and crosses her legs*) Do I look ten years old to you?

Stevenson No. Slightly older.

Monica And you don't look sixty-four.

Stevenson Don't tell me I look slightly older.

Monica Not in this light.

Stevenson Thank heavens for that. I feel a hundred and four.

Monica You're not Grandad Fogerty, are you?

Stevenson (*sitting beside him*) Listen, Monica, can you keep a secret?

Monica Nothing escapes my lips.

Stevenson Yes, well. You know there's a war on?

Monica Course I do. I've seen it on the newsreels.

Stevenson Well, you know that some people don't like fighting and getting shot at?

Monica Mum says men should be proud to be shot at.

Stevenson Not everybody shares your mum's views, Monica.

Monica (*smiling*) I get it.

Stevenson You do? How often?

Monica You're hiding here until the war's ended.

Stevenson Go to the top of the class.

Monica That's real keen.

Stevenson You think so?

Monica Yes. I'm going to be staying here until it ends, too.

Stevenson You are?

Monica Yes. (*Rising*) Mum thinks a young, sweet schoolgirl like me is in grave moral danger back home, especially with all those Yankee GI's roaming around.

Stevenson So she's brought you here?

Monica That's right. (*Giggling*) Where there aren't any nasty young men.

Stevenson I think we ought to drink a toast to good old mum.

Monica What with?

Stevenson (*conspiritorially*) Ah. Ah ... (*He takes a flagon of muddy looking liquid out from under the bed*) Home-made carrot wine. I've got the apparatus for making it under the bed.

Monica Keen.

Stevenson Here's to a long drawn out war.

He drinks and gives the flagon to Monica

Monica Here's to Mr Hitler for starting it all. (*Staying her hand as she goes to drink, smiling*)

Stevenson Wait a minute. You're not under the age to be partaking of strong liquor, are you?

Monica Cheeky. (*She smiles and takes a drink*) Mmm ... I never knew there were such clever uses for a carrot. (*She takes another gulp*)

Stevenson I think I ought to warn you that stuff is pretty potent.

Monica What about you?

Stevenson I'm pretty potent, too.

Monica (*seductively*) I think you are all talk.

Stevenson I think you'd better sit down.

Monica Why?

Stevenson Take another sip and you'll see.

Monica (*taking a gulp and swaying slightly*) Phew.

Stevenson I warned you.

Monica This has got a kick like a French mule skinner.

Stevenson You know why?

Monica (*sitting beside Stevenson on the bed*) *Mais non, monsieur.*

Stevenson (*interested*) You can speak French?

Monica *Voulez-vous coucher avec moi, monsieur?*

Stevenson That's great. (*Picking up a book*) Can you translate this for me?

Monica But I can't speak French.

Stevenson But I just heard you.

Monica That's all I know.

Stevenson (*disappointedly*) Oh great.

Monica (*drinking*) But Pierre can probably help you.

Stevenson Pierre?

Monica Mum's latest boyfriend. He's very high in the French consulate.

Stevenson He's no good to me in the French consulate.

Monica But he's here.

Stevenson Here? On this island?

Monica (*giving the flagon to Stevenson*) Yes.

Stevenson (*drinking*) Great. (*Having second thoughts*) No ... He'll give me away.

Monica No he won't.

Stevenson I can't risk it.

Monica He's very anxious to meet Grandad.

Stevenson Why?

Monica No idea.

Stevenson He'll find that a trifle difficult.

Monica (*brightly*) Couldn't you pretend you're Grandad?

Stevenson (*sarcastically*) Oh sure. I'd really fool him.

Monica You nearly fooled me.

Stevenson But you're not a French diplomat.

Monica What's so important about a few stuffy old books, anyway?

Stevenson It's driving me mad having all these sexy books around and not being able to get so much as a tingle out of them.

Monica (*taking the book from Stevenson and placing it on the floor; overtly sensual*) But, *chéri* ... you have me.

Stevenson But you can't read French.

Monica I know, but I can make you tingle.

Stevenson (*hesitantly*) I'm sure you can, Monica. I, well ... I ... It's just that ...
Monica Don't I appeal to you?
Stevenson Yes, you do. But ...
Monica (*kissing him*) Well then?
Stevenson It's just, well ... Your outfit.
Monica It bothers you?
Stevenson A bit. It makes me feel like a ...
Monica (*smiling and standing*) I understand. Easily solved. (*She begins to disrobe*)
Stevenson (*gulping his wine*) You know, they do say carrot wine is very good for the eyesight.
Monica Is that so?
Stevenson Yes.
Monica What else do they say? (*She stands in her underwear*)
Stevenson They say good eyesight isn't everything—but it comes in handy.

Monica dives under the blankets with Stevenson

Monica (*singing*) "Oh! Oh! Oh! What a lovely war ..."

Mildred enters R *into the main area. She now wears a different, more appealing dressing-gown. She carries Stevenson's clothes and is singing "The Man I Love". She is followed by Adele who pursues her urgently. She has a towel with which she dries herself*

Adele (*impatiently*) Mrs Fogerty, have you listened to any word I've said?
Mildred (*going to the door* US) Of course I have, dear.
Adele But have you understood any of it?
Mildred (*stopping at the door*) Not quite all of it.
Adele (*sighing*) Which part can't you understand?
Mildred Why you should want to see my Alfred.
Adele I've explained all that.
Mildred I'm still a little confused.
Adele Look, your darling Alfred is an enemy agent.
Mildred (*leaving the door and smiling indulgently*) Really, Miss——
Adele Dumbrovski. Adele Dumbrovski.
Mildred Really, Miss—— you don't expect me to believe that.
Adele You've got to believe it.
Mildred But it's not possible.
Adele Look, every minute that passes could be fatal.
Mildred You Americans have such vivid imaginations.
Adele And you Limeys can be so infuriatingly blasé.
Mildred No need to be crude.
Adele Can't you get it through your head? Once your husband meets up with Maurice Latoule it's really going to be on for young and old.
Mildred On?
Adele Fireworks. Pow. Zap. Ker-chow.
Mildred Why should I believe anything you say, anyway?
Adele Because I work for American Intelligence.

Mildred So you said. But you haven't any proof of that.

Adele I haven't any credentials because there aren't any pockets in swim-suits.

Mildred Ah, well, there you are. You could be a Scottish Nationalist for all I know.

Adele Mrs Fogerty, where *is* your husband?

Mildred He's gone fishing.

Adele Whose clothes are they?

Mildred Er—mine.

Adele (*snatching the underpants from Mildred and holding them up*) Yours?

Mildred (*snatching the underpants back*) Yes.

Adele What's through that door?

Mildred Storeroom.

Adele It leads to the top of the lighthouse, doesn't it?

Mildred No.

Adele Does.

Mildred Doesn't.

Adele Does.

Mildred Doesn't.

Adele Well, we'll see. (*She tries the upstage door. It is locked*)

Mildred Why don't you go back where you came from and leave us alone?

Adele Gimme the key.

Mildred (*backing away*) Haven't got one.

Adele Have.

Mildred Haven't.

Adele Have.

Mildred Haven't.

Adele Have.

Adele lunges at Mildred. After a slight struggle she takes a key from Mildred's dressing-gown pocket. Mildred drops the clothes

(*Triumphantly*) Ha, ha. Have. (*She rushes to the upstage door*)

Mildred chases her, grabs back the key and backs away

(*Advancing on Mildred*) Mrs Fogerty, gimme the key.

Mildred No.

Adele Yes.

Mildred No.

Adele Yes, you deranged old hag.

Mildred No, you bitchy little trollop.

Adele Yes, you vaporous half-wit.

Mildred No, you ... you ... droopy drawers.

Mildred exits hurriedly R

Adele (*giving chase*) So help me ... when I catch you ...

Adele exits R

The door L opens slowly. Detective Sergeant Walter Tomkins suddenly bursts into the room. He is middle-aged, precise and humourless. He holds a gun

Tomkins (*looking suspiciously round the room*) All right, Constable. The place is deserted. I don't think they know we're here, though. My idea to land the boat on the other side of the island was a stroke of genius. All the same, we'd better be prepared for violence. Better let me have the bullet. (*He holds out his hand behind him. On getting no response he turns to find no-one there; angrily*) Constable Holmes! Will you get in here? I know what you're up to.

Holmes enters L. He wears plain clothes, is in his thirties and is fun-loving

Holmes (*with a big smile*) What am I up to, Sarge?

Tomkins *Sergeant Tomkins.* I won't tell you how to address me again.

Holmes OK. What am I up to, Sergeant Tomkins?

Tomkins You don't fool me. Wipe that lipstick off your disgusting face. And tell Miss Lane it's safe to enter now.

Holmes (*wiping off the lipstick; calling through the door L*) Gloria, the sarge says——

Gloria (*off*) I know, I know. I heard him.

Gloria Lane enters L. She is in her thirties, flashy and common. She wears shorts, a blouse and sandals

God. What have we here? Shipwrecks Anonymous?

Tomkins This is where we finally get what we're after.

Holmes As the actress said to the bishop.

Tomkins (*seething*) I won't warn you again, Constable. I've had just about enough of your crudities.

Holmes (*smiling*) Sorry, Sergeant Tomkins.

Tomkins Have some respect for Miss Lane here.

Gloria Don't mind me, lovey.

Tomkins You've had enough harrowing experiences, my dear ... er ... Miss Lane ... without the police force adding to your worries.

Gloria (*sitting on a crate*) Yes, I have, haven't I?

Tomkins How are you bearing up?

Gloria (*taking off her sandals and rubbing her feet*) Knackered. Did we *have* to indulge in a hundred mile route march to get here?

Holmes The sergeant believes in the element of surprise. Don't you, Sergeant Tomkins?

Gloria Well, he certainly surprised me. I thought we were going to have a nice seaside jaunt. I brought my suntan lotion.

Holmes (*sitting beside Gloria*) Would you like me to rub it on for you?

Tomkins (*bristling*) Constable Holmes!

Gloria Oh leave him alone. He's only being thoughtful. (*Patting Holmes' cheek*) Aren't you, sweetie?

Holmes (*smiling*) All in a day's duty, ma'am.

Tomkins Holmes, I shudder to think what will happen to you when my report gets in.

Gloria Oh, shove your report.

Tomkins (*shocked*) Miss Lane!

Gloria And if there's room for your truncheon, shove that too.

Holmes can barely hide a smile

Tomkins You seem to have forgotten that I have devoted the best part of the last two years to your interests, Miss Lane.

Gloria With a hell of a lot of lack of success, it seems to me.

Tomkins We're closing in now.

Holmes Sergeant Tomkins always gets his man. Don't you, Sergeant Tomkins?

Tomkins They don't call me Tenacity Tomkins for nothing.

Holmes No. He pays them ten pounds a week.

Tomkins (*containing himself with difficulty*) My report on you is looking bleaker by the minute, Holmes.

Holmes *Sergeant* Holmes.

Tomkins *Constable* Holmes.

Holmes I'm a sergeant now.

Tomkins Only temporarily.

Holmes Temporarily or not, I'd like to be called Sergeant Holmes.

Gloria (*to Holmes*) John.

Holmes Yes, Gloria?

Gloria Leave off, will you? Don't get him going.

Holmes (*putting his hand on Gloria's knee*) Did you bring your swimming costume with you, petal?

Gloria Yes. Did you?

Holmes No.

Gloria Never mind. You can skinny dip.

Holmes I will if you will.

Tomkins (*exploding*) This is too much!

Holmes As the actress said to the bishop.

Tomkins Will you take your hand off that young lady's ... er ... off her ...

Gloria I think it's called a knee.

Tomkins Thank you for the anatomy lesson. I know what it is and a police officer on duty has no right to have his hand on it.

Gloria Why, Walter, I do believe you're jealous.

Tomkins (*stiffly*) Miss Lane, must I remind you of the nature of our presence here?

Gloria After two years I think I've forgotten.

Tomkins Then let me refresh your memory.

Gloria Do you ever stop being a copper?

Tomkins (*unheeding*) We are here to apprehend one Alfred Fogerty. You are here to bear witness to the fact that the same Alfred Fogerty did assault you, Gloria Lane, on February the fourteenth, nineteen forty-two in an air raid shelter in Liverpool, with intent to rape. And that——

Holmes We don't know that for sure, Sarge.

Tomkins glowers

Sergeant Tomkins.

Tomkins (*scornfully*) As you have so very succinctly pointed out in your best, erudite fashion, we do not know that for sure—Constable. No doubt you may have noticed the presence of Miss Lane, the unfortunate victim, on our visit here?

Holmes (*looking at Gloria*) I've noticed her, yes.

Tomkins You've got your filthy hands on her every time my back's turned. (*He turns his back*)

Holmes grabs Gloria and kisses her neck. Gloria giggles. Tomkins swings around. Holmes releases his hold and he and Gloria look up innocently at Tomkins

Constable Holmes, will you get away from that young lady?

Holmes But she needs my protection.

Tomkins She needs your protection like she needs a dose of the 'flu.

Gloria Can I say something?

Tomkins (*to Holmes*) Miss Lane is here to identify her assailant——

Holmes I know that. All I'm saying is——

Tomkins Don't interrupt.

Gloria Can I say something?

Holmes Fogerty might not be the assailant.

Tomkins He's our man all right.

Holmes We don't know that for sure.

Gloria Can I say something?

Tomkins (*to Holmes*) When you've been in the force as long as I have——

Gloria (*standing on a crate*) Listen! My bones ache, my feet throb and my legs feel like concertinas, thanks to the little ramble you brought me on. Do you think we could find somebody to make us a cup of tea, at least?

Mildred enters R

Mildred (*aghast*) Good gracious! Where'd you all spring from?

Tomkins swings round, instinctively produces his gun and points it at Mildred

(*Fearfully*) Oh dear. Please don't.

Holmes (*to Tomkins*) Do you want the bullet, Sarge?

Tomkins puts the gun in his pocket. He approaches Mildred

Tomkins No cause for alarm, madam.

Mildred (*calming down*) You've already alarmed me.

Tomkins I'm sorry about that, madam. You see——

Mildred (*going to Gloria; aggrieved*) Do you stand round on your furniture at home, young lady? If you do then your mother should smack your bottom for it.

Completely fazed, Gloria gets off and moves L. Mildred takes a rag from her pocket and wipes the top of the crate. She pushes Holmes out of the way. He moves R to join Tomkins. All watch Mildred fascinated

Tomkins (*breaking the silence*) Are you Mildred Fogerty?

Mildred I'm not answering any questions until I've seen my solicitor. (*She continues to dust round the room*)

Tomkins I'm Sergeant Tomkins and this is Constable Holmes. (*He shows her his credentials*)

Mildred peers at them and continues dusting

We'd like to talk to Mr Fogerty.

Mildred studiously ignores him as she dusts

(*Getting impatient*) Where is Mr Fogerty?
Gloria I think she's slightly deaf.
Tomkins I think she's slightly batty.
Holmes (*to Mildred, with a disarming smile*) Mrs Fogerty—Mildred. This is just a mere routine inquiry. Nothing to get worked up about. You're not in any trouble. I mean, why should you be? No need to worry about a thing. All we want to do is ask your husband some questions. Some tiny infinitesimal questions. Really miniscule, almost totally non-existent questions. In fact, I don't know why we're bothering to ask the questions at all. They're so . . . so——
Mildred (*dusting the radio*) Can you fix up my wireless?
Holmes Pardon?
Mildred This thing. It always used to cough a bit, especially when *Workers' Playtime* was on. But now it won't come out with anything. Can you fix it for me?
Holmes I'm sorry, but we have an arrangement with the radio repair people. We don't repair radios and they don't arrest people.

Pierre Dubois enters L. *He is out of breath*

Pierre I can find your husband nowhere. I have—— (*He stops as he sees company*)

Tomkins approaches him quickly as Pierre turns to exit

Tomkins One moment, sir. I'd like to ask you a few questions.
Pierre (*agitatedly*) But . . . I don't understand.
Tomkins (*showing his credentials*) Police.
Pierre (*more agitatedly*) Police? But I do nothing.
Tomkins Don't be alarmed, sir.
Pierre I tell you, you make mistake. (*Pointing at Mildred*) Whatever she has told you is a lie. Big lie. I know nothing of Vichy. I hate Vichy. (*He spits in disgust*) That to Vichy. Vive General de Gaulle.
Tomkins (*to Gloria*) Is this the man?

Gloria goes up to Pierre. She eyes him approvingly

Gloria Well . . . (*She walks around Pierre*)
Pierre (*nonplussed*) Who is she?
Mildred She's a very naughty girl.
Gloria It *was* dark.
Tomkins I know, but you said you'd recognize him again.
Gloria Not with his clothes on.

Pierre becomes alarmed. He tries to dash through the door but Holmes bars his way. Pierre backs wildly around the room

Holmes Come now, sir; no cause for alarm.
Pierre You English are all perverted pigs.
Mildred I think you should co-operate, Luigi.
Pierre I have my dignity.
Gloria Come on, it's only a little thing.
Holmes That's not what you told us.
Mildred I say, isn't this exciting?
Pierre Keep away from me, you fiends.
Mildred I always said that justice should be seen to be done.

Holmes grabs hold of Pierre. Everyone except Tomkins advances on him

Tomkins (*with great authority*) Hold it. Everybody hold it.

All stop in their tracks

Pierre (*desperately*) Please, Monsieur Policeman, don't say that.
Tomkins (*to Mildred*) Did you call him Luigi?
Mildred Yes. That's his name.
Tomkins (*to Pierre*) You are *not* Alfred Fogerty, resident of this lighthouse?
Pierre (*angrily*) I am Pierre Dubois and I am an important member of the French consulate in London.
Tomkins Are you getting everything down, Constable Holmes?

Pierre instinctively holds on to his trousers as Holmes moves his hand

Holmes (*taking out his notebook and pencil*) How do you spell your last name, sir?
Pierre Never mind. This outrage shall be reported to the authorities.
Gloria I knew there was something not right. It's the accent.
Holmes Yes. It sounds phoney to me too.
Gloria No. I mean, Fogerty didn't have a French accent.
Holmes I thought you said he only grunted and gasped.
Gloria He did. But in English.
Holmes (*to Pierre*) Let's hear you grunt and gasp, sir.
Pierre I will do no such thing. (*To Tomkins*) This is monstrous, monsieur. When I have finished with you, you will be riding a bicycle in Balham.
Tomkins (*placating*) Now, now, sir. No hard feelings.
Holmes As the actress said to——
Tomkins (*glaring*) Holmes! (*To Pierre*) A natural mistake, sir. We thought the only man living on this island was Alfred Fogerty.
Pierre I do not live here.
Holmes They why are you here?
Tomkins I'll ask the questions, thank you.
Gloria Then ask him why he's here.
Tomkins (*to Pierre*) Why are you here?
Pierre I do not have to answer your questions. I am diplomatically immune.

Daphne enters L in great agitation

Daphne I can't find her anywhere. I'm so worried——

Daphne stops as she sees a room full of people turn to her

(*Pointing at Tomkins and Holmes; with a strangled cry*) Men! (*She sits on a tea-chest to recover*)

Holmes (*advancing to Daphne; to Tomkins*) Shall I examine her to see if it's Fogerty in disguise?

Tomkins Control your zeal, Constable.

Holmes Well, you never know.

Daphne This place is infested with them.

Gloria With what? Flies?

Daphne With men.

Gloria (*interested*) Oh? Really?

Mildred And they've all got flies.

Daphne I just wish I could find Monica so that I can keep her away from them.

Tomkins (*showing his credentials*) Police. Who are you?

Daphne I'm a caring mother, but that wouldn't matter to you, would it? (*She sobs pathetically*)

Tomkins (*appealing to everyone*) Will someone please enlighten me as to the identity of this female person?

Mildred She's my daughter, Annabelle.

Pierre Her name is Daphne Delgrado.

Holmes Delgrado? Sounds like another bleeding foreigner to me.

Pierre She is married to an Italian.

Tomkins (*knowingly*) I see. (*To Daphne*) Excuse me, miss.

Daphne continues sobbing

(*Raising his voice*) I said—excuse me, miss.

Daphne sobs louder. Gloria sits next to her and puts her arms around her

Gloria Come on now, Daphne. Don't let Genghis Khan upset you.

Tomkins Miss Lane——

Gloria Why don't you stop bullying people?

Tomkins All I said was——

Gloria (*to Daphne*) Who's Monica?

Daphne My little girl.

Gloria Is she lost?

Daphne Yes.

Gloria Don't worry, love. We'll find her. (*To Tomkins*) Won't we?

Tomkins Well, I . . . I don't think . . .

Gloria (*to Daphne*) When did you last see her?

Daphne About half an hour ago. She was down by the jetty playing with her shuttlecock.

Gloria (*springing to her feet*) Right then.

Tomkins Right then what?

Gloria Organize a search party. (*To Daphne*) You're very lucky the police are here. They're very clever at finding lost kids.

Tomkins Now just hang on a minute, Miss Lane——
Gloria There isn't a second to lose.
Tomkins I'm in charge here.
Gloria Then get things moving.
Holmes Good for you, Gloria.
Tomkins (*glaring at Holmes*) I'm not here to go looking for wandering kids.

Daphne sobs loudly

Mildred Callous.
Pierre Unfeeling cochon.
Gloria Supercilious sod.
Daphne Rapist.
Holmes (*to Tomkins*) I think we'd better look for the little girl, Sarge.
Tomkins (*flustered*) She's probably having a lovely time with her shuttle-cock somewhere.
Mildred Probably drowned.
Pierre Or lost.
Gloria Or injured.
Daphne Or raped.
Holmes I think we'd better look for the little girl, Sarge.
Tomkins All right! All right! Mrs Fogerty, you and I will look by the jetty, Monsieur and Daphne look south, Constable Holmes and Miss Lane look—no, Miss Lane better come with me.
Gloria I'll go with Mr Pierre.
Holmes You'd be better off with me.
Gloria But he's a Frenchman.
Holmes So what?
Gloria They have an instinct for these things.
Holmes I know what they have an instinct for, and it isn't for search parties.
Gloria (*smiling*) I do believe you're jealous.
Holmes (*offended*) I am not jealous. I just don't think——
Mildred Luigi should come with me.
Daphne No, he shouldn't. He should come with me.
Gloria Me.
Mildred Me.
Daphne He's mine. He comes with me.
Pierre (*honoured*) Please, ladies, I must do what the sergeant suggests.
Tomkins That's right. Monsieur Frenchman goes with Constable Holmes.

Pierre and Holmes look disappointed

Miss Lane with me, and Mrs Fogerty with Mrs Delgrado.

Gloria	⎫	I want to be with Pierre
Daphne	⎪	I'm not going with her.
Holmes	⎬ (*together*)	I should go with Gloria.
Pierre	⎪	Daphne should be with me.
Mildred	⎭	I'm not going with her.

Tomkins (*with great authority*) I have spoken.
Holmes You're the boss.

Tomkins I'm glad you accept that. I do have a certain flair for these things.
Holmes As the actress said to the bishop.
Tomkins My report on you will be abysmal.
Daphne (*tearfully*) Will somebody do something?
Tomkins Right! Er . . . what does your daughter look like?
Daphne She's a young schoolgirl, virginal and sweet.
Tomkins (*to Mildred*) I don't suppose you have a bloodhound?
Mildred No. But I used to have a hamster.
Holmes (*to Tomkins*) But, Sarge, what about Alfred Fogerty?
Mildred He wouldn't make a very good bloodhound. No sense of smell whatsoever.
Tomkins (*self importantly*) Fogerty can wait. We have other, more immediate duties to perform.

Tomkins exits L, *followed by the others. Mildred is the last to exit. She closes the door*

In the top part of the lighthouse Stevenson stirs. He looks at Monica, who is sound asleep.

Stevenson (*shaking Monica*) Monica. Monica . . . come on. Wakey, wakey. (*He shakes her hard*)

She remains asleep

No more carrot wine for you. Listen, sweetie-pie, I think you should put in an appearance down below. Monica . . . Monica . . . your mum will be worried about you.

He shakes Monica but she stays asleep

You can't stay here. You'll have to—— (*He sees Monica's school uniform on the floor. His face lights up. Putting on the uniform*) Don't worry about a thing, Monica. You stay there as long as you like—you take it easy. My need is greater than yours.

Finally dressed, Stevenson climbs through the window and exits

As he disappears from view, Monica wakes up and looks around

Monica Lover boy . . . where are you? (*She goes to get her clothes and finds they are missing*) Well, of all the nerve. (*She sits on the bed, sees the flagon and takes a drink*)

In the main area, the door opens R *and Adele enters. She is bound hand and foot and gagged. She hops about the room wildly. She hops to the door* L, *cannot open it and hops back through the door* R

Pause

Stevenson enters R *in Monica's uniform. He peers cautiously into the room. He sees his own clothes and goes to them. He stops abruptly as he hears voices. He looks around the room. He goes towards the door* R

Stevenson Mildred? Is anybody else here?

Tomkins (*off*) I assure you, Miss Lane, she went in there.
Gloria (*off*) Are you sure? I didn't see her.

Stevenson becomes worried. He looks around for a hiding place. He jumps into the crate UL *and closes the lid*

Tomkins and Gloria enter L

(*Looking around*) Told you. There's no schoolgirl in here. You're seeing things.

Tomkins suddenly grabs her and throws her on to the crate hiding Stevenson

Tomkins (*passionately*) Oh, Miss Lane, I just had to get you alone.
Gloria Sergeant Tomkins, what's come over you?
Tomkins Love, Miss Lane, love, passion, and overwhelming desire to possess you.
Gloria All right. But aren't you on duty?
Tomkins (*holding her close*) Sometimes a man has a duty to himself.
Gloria Sergeant Tomkins——
Tomkins Call me Walter.
Gloria Walter, you have a wife and five children.
Tomkins They don't understand me.
Gloria I think I do.
Tomkins That's what I like about you, you're so . . . so . . .
Gloria Available?
Tomkins (*kissing her passionately*) Oh, Gloria, I've longed for this moment.

Tomkins lies on top of Gloria on the crate and embraces her

Adele hops out of the door R *to stand behind the pair. She strains to make her presence felt by making noises and hopping; but to no avail*

Mildred enters L. *She carries a basket of carrots. She sees Adele, puts the basket on the floor, rushes to her and grabs her. She puts Adele in a crate* UR, *closes the lid and sits on the crate. She watches Tomkins and Gloria*

Holmes, Daphne and Pierre enter L

Holmes Mrs Delgrado said she saw——

Tomkins and Gloria break from the clinch

Tomkins Yes, Constable, what were you saying?
Holmes Er . . . Mrs Delgrado said she saw a young girl come in here.
Tomkins (*slightly embarrassed*) I think she was mistaken, Constable.
Daphne I thought I saw Monica's uniform.
Pierre So did I.

Adele's muffled cries are heard

Holmes What's that?
Mildred What?
Holmes It sounded like muffled cries.

In the top part of the lighthouse, Monica puts down the flagon and climbs through the window

Pierre I heard it too.

Tomkins Why aren't you all out looking for that poor little schoolgirl?

Daphne We saw her come in here.

Tomkins She didn't.

Pierre How can you be sure?

Tomkins Because Miss Lane and I would have seen her.

Mildred I came in and you didn't see me.

Tomkins (*nonplussed*) Well, I ... er ... I was carrying out a routine inspection.

Mildred That's some routine you've got.

Adele's muffled cries are heard

Holmes What's that?

Mildred What?

Holmes You haven't got some sort of stomach complaint, have you?

Pierre I think funny noises come from that crate.

Mildred Why don't you shut up, Mr——

Pierre Dubois.

Gloria I can hear something too.

Daphne (*wandering around the room*) Perhaps it's my little Monica. Perhaps she's here somewhere, trying to get some message to her loving, caring mother and unable to because of some terrible barrier that has been placed between us. Perhaps Monica is trying to tell me she needs me, she's in trouble, she's been a victim of some terrible fate, she's——

All Oh, shut up!

Monica enters L. *She is in her underwear and so tipsy she is almost asleep*

Monica Did anybody see my demon lover pass this way?

Daphne (*shocked*) Monica. Where's your uniform?

All go to Monica. Daphne embraces her. Mildred leaves the crate and crosses to Monica. Adele jumps up from the crate. She hops over to the others as they gather round Monica. She tries desperately to make her presence felt. Mildred is the first to see her. She tries to usher a protesting Adele back through door R. *Tomkins sees them*

Tomkins (*to Mildred*) Who is that person?

Mildred (*pulling up*) Person? What person?

Tomkins The one in swimsuit and ropes.

Holmes Maybe I should examine her to see if she's Fogerty in disguise. (*He goes to Adele*)

Tomkins Just remove her constraints, Constable.

Holmes takes off Adele's ropes. He takes the gag off her last

Adele For Chrissake, will someone listen to me before all hell breaks loose?

CURTAIN

ACT II

The same. Seconds later

When the CURTAIN *rises everyone is in the same positions as at the end of* ACT I

Tomkins (*to Adele*) Would you like to repeat that?

Adele Certainly. For Chrissake, will someone listen to me before all hell breaks loose?

Pierre (*agitatedly*) Why, surely it isn't . . . Could it be? Why, it is. It's Adele. Sacre bleu.

Adele (*unfriendly*) Don't sacred blue me, you . . . you . . . vicious Vichyite. You louse . . . you . . . you . . .

Pierre (*going to Adele*) Why, ma petite petal, after all these years.

Adele Whadya mean? It's only a few days——

Pierre (*taking her in his arms*) It only seems a few days to me too.

Adele (*squirming*) Don't sweet talk me. I'm on to you, and your little plan.

Monica lies on the crate containing Stevenson. She is in a daze

Daphne Pierre, who is this . . . female?

Adele His name isn't Pierre, it's——

Pierre (*in a half whisper*) Adele, ma sweet. I do not think you should say too much.

Adele I'm blowing the whistle on you, Maurice Latoule.

Pierre (*putting his arms around her; charmingly*) I think you had better not, sugar plum. You would regret it.

Adele Why?

Pierre Put your hand in my pocket and take out what you find there.

Adele goes to put her hand in Pierre's pocket

My back pocket.

Adele takes some photos from Pierre's back pocket. She studies them in growing concern as she moves UR

Tomkins Will someone explain to me what's going on?

Mildred I thought *you* were the detective.

Daphne (*to Monica*) I'd like to know where your clothes are.

Monica smiles sleepily

Holmes I think I know what's going on.

Gloria (*sitting on a tea-chest*) You're a better man than I am, Rin Tin Tin.

Tomkins (*to Holmes*) We're not interested in your wild conjectures, Constable.

Daphne (*to Monica*) Say something, child.

Monica (*smiling sleepily*) Carrots, lovely carrots.

Gloria (*to Mildred*) Is there anywhere in this madhouse where I can get cleaned up and lie down?

Mildred But aren't you leaving?

Tomkins We're leaving when our mission is accomplished.

Holmes On present progress that will be when Lord Nelson gets his eye back.

Tomkins I'm warning you . . .

Gloria (*to Mildred*) Lead on, MacTavish.

Mildred (*worried*) Oh dear.

Mildred exits R, *taking the basket of carrots. Gloria follows*

Adele looks at the photos wide-eyed. Pierre watches her amused. Daphne tries to arouse Monica. Holmes assists her. Tomkins sees Stevenson's clothes and picks them up

Tomkins Who belongs to these?

Pierre (*to Adele*) Interesting, non?

Adele (*fuming*) You creep . . . you lousy——

Pierre Now, now, Adele, ma sweet, that is no way to speak to someone who has been so good to you.

Adele (*scathingly*) Good to me? Ha!

Tomkins I said, who belongs to these?

Holmes (*to Daphne*) I think she may have what is known as lighthouse delirium.

Daphne What can we do?

Holmes Loosen her clothing.

Daphne But she hasn't got any.

Holmes Then we'd better give her some air. I'll take her outside.

Daphne *We'll* take her outside.

Holmes Good idea.

Tomkins Will someone tell me who belongs to these?

Holmes and Daphne take Monica towards the door L

Monica (*half conscious*) I don't even know your name.

Holmes Call me John. John Holmes, at your service.

Monica (*giggling drunkenly*) Johnny, Johnny, quite contrary, how do your carrots grow? With silver bells, and——

Holmes and Daphne take Monica through the door L

Tomkins Constable Holmes! (*He throws the clothing on the floor*)

Tomkins dashes through the door L

Adele is left glowering at Pierre

Pierre (*smarmily*) Well, what do you think?

Adele You know what I think of you.

Pierre (*taking the photos from her*) I mean these lovely snapshots.

Adele Think you're clever, don't you?

Pierre Please, no flattery.

Adele I'd no idea there was a guy with a camera sharing our romantic moments.

Pierre I felt it was a necessary precaution, under the circumstances.

Adele He didn't get my best side.

Pierre I think you show up rather well.

Adele But I only ... did those things so that I could get the low down on you and your rotten URGE.

Pierre I know.

Adele It was all in the line of duty.

Pierre I know. Duty to Uncle Sam and the cause.

Adele OK, Maurice. What do you want from me?

Pierre First of all, my name is not Maurice.

Adele OK. It's Pierre. Go on.

Pierre Quite simple, my little marzipan. You do not, how you say? blow the whistle on me, and your loving, trusting husband and children do not learn of your hitherto unknown talents.

Adele You think I'd risk a whole convoy of allied ships being wiped out, maybe lead to us losing the war and fascism ruling the world in order to protect my reputation?

Pierre Yes.

Adele OK. But I'll always hate you for this.

Pierre I am glad we understand each other.

Adele What about this Fogerty guy? Or should I say codename Mustard-seed? Code number two-nine-one-o-six-seven?

Pierre What about him?

Adele You obviously haven't met up with the treacherous pig yet.

Pierre I will.

Adele Time's running out fast. That convoy will be on the horizon before you can say Amos 'n' Andy.

Pierre I am aware of that.

Adele Why don't you give up?

Pierre He can only be in one place. At the top of the lighthouse.

Adele He isn't up there. I've looked.

Pierre I think you are lying, Mrs Dumbrovski.

Adele Anyway, you'll never get up there. His wife will see to that, believe me.

Pierre I have not come this far to be baulked at the last hurdle.

Adele We'll see. (*She sees Stevenson's clothes and picks them up*) It's time I got dressed. Wrong sex but who cares? (*She goes to the door* L)

Pierre Adele, we have a bargain. Right?

Adele Yeah, yeah. You'd better get back to Daphne, lover boy, before she comes looking for you.

Adele exits R. *Pierre thinks for a moment, tries the door to the top of the lighthouse, then exits* L

The lid to the crate UL *slowly opens and Stevenson cautiously climbs out looking dazed. He goes to where his clothes were and pulls up as he finds them missing. He searches frantically around the room.*

Stevenson They've got to be here somewhere. What have I done to deserve this? The army can't be worse than this. The woman's a raving nutcase. Why should I stay here? What's this place got to keep me here? (*Thinking*) Monica, that's what. (*Smiling*) I think it might be worth the sacrifice.

Mildred enters R. *She wears a more gaudy dressing-gown*

Mildred (*singing*) "You'd be so easy to love, so . . ."

She sees Stevenson, who turns to face her

Young girl, there's such a thing as knocking before entering a person's home.
Stevenson This *is* my home.
Mildred And don't be cheeky.
Stevenson Mildred, where are my clothes?
Mildred (*slowly recognizing him*) Malcolm?
Stevenson Yes.
Mildred Are you sure?
Stevenson Positive. I want something to wear.
Mildred You *are* wearing something.
Stevenson I'm not getting around like this forever, even for you.
Mildred I like your hat.
Stevenson (*his patience waning*) Listen, has everyone left the island yet?
Mildred I don't think so.
Stevenson Then I'd better keep myself scarce. Get me some of Alfred's clothes.
Mildred But they don't fit you.
Stevenson I know that. Get some anyway.
Mildred I don't think you should talk to me like that, Malcolm.
Stevenson (*his patience gone*) Get them. Now. And give me the key to the tower.
Mildred (*uncertainly*) Well . . .
Stevenson I'll give it back to you. Anyway, you have a spare key.

Mildred takes the key from her pocket

Mildred Well . . .

Stevenson snatches the key

Stevenson (*earnestly*) Listen, Mildred, did you know Alfred was a traitor?
Mildred A trader? What trade was he in?
Stevenson (*sighing*) He was working for the enemy. He was supposed to meet up with one of them today to sabotage the lighthouse.
Mildred How do you know that?
Stevenson I've just heard an interesting conversation. I want you to do one thing for me. Let Pierre up to see me. Leave the door unlocked.
Mildred But you're not supposed to be here.

Stevenson I'll pretend I'm Alfred. Tell him I've got some great elixir or something that makes me young. He'll believe you.

Mildred (*doubting*) I don't know ...

Stevenson I'm going to be a hero out of this. Malcolm Stevenson saves democracy for the world.

Mildred I don't know, Malcolm. They might take you away from me.

Stevenson I know. We'd just have to grin and bear it. Now get those clothes — please.

Mildred (*shaking her head*) I don't like it. I don't like it at all.

Mildred exits R

Stevenson unlocks the upstage door and opens it

Holmes enters L

Holmes Hello, hello. Who have we here, then?

Stevenson (*in a girlish voice*) Oh, hello.

Holmes (*friendly*) Where've you been hiding?

Stevenson I ... er ... I ... er ...

Holmes Is that the door to the top of the lighthouse?

Stevenson Er ... yes.

Holmes Just come down, have you?

Stevenson Er ... yes.

Holmes And who might you be then?

Stevenson I'm ... er ... Mr and Mrs Fogerty's little granddaughter.

Holmes Another one?

Stevenson Yes. Annabelle's side of things.

Holmes Well, well.

Stevenson (*moving through the door*) Well, it's been lovely meeting you.

Holmes takes Stevenson's arm and leads him C

Holmes No need to go yet, sweetheart. I'm a policeman.

Stevenson Oh, how marvellous for you.

Holmes Perhaps you can help me.

Stevenson I don't think I can.

Holmes Well, we'll see. (*Taking out his notebook*) What's your name, darling?

Stevenson (*coyly*) I'd rather not say.

Holmes Come on now. No-one's going to hurt you.

Stevenson Promise?

Holmes Promise. Do you like barley sugar?

Stevenson No, I don't.

Holmes (*surprised*) Really? I thought all young girls liked barley sugar.

Stevenson Do they? Oh, sorry, I thought you said wine gums.

Holmes Just tell me your name and you can have a stick.

Stevenson Of what?

Holmes Barley sugar.

Stevenson Oh. Er ... My name's Susan.

Holmes (*writing*) Susan what?

Stevenson Hardcastle.
Holmes Right, Susan. Is your grandfather up there?
Stevenson No.
Holmes (*smiling*) Tell the truth now.
Stevenson Honest, he isn't.
Holmes Cross your heart and hope to die?
Stevenson I'm telling the truth. (*He crosses his heart*)
Holmes Well, it's not that I don't believe you, Susan, but I think I'll just check to make sure. (*He goes to the upstage door*)
Stevenson Oh, Mr Policeman?
Holmes Yes?
Stevenson You won't tell anybody you saw me, will you?
Holmes Why? Are you a big secret?
Stevenson It's just that—I'm playing truant from school.
Holmes (*shaking his head*) You naughty thing, you. You'll never get anywhere if you miss school.

Holmes exits upstage. Mildred enters R *carrying a bundle of clothes*

Mildred (*singing*) "I can't give you anything but love, baby. That's . . ." (*To Stevenson*) I thought you were going upstairs.
Stevenson (*taking the clothes from Mildred*) There's a cop up there.
Mildred They're everywhere.
Stevenson (*going to the door* R) I'll change in there.
Mildred There's a woman in there having a bath. And another one wearing your clothes.
Stevenson (*astounded*) Wearing my—— Are you mad?
Mildred Me mad? I'm not the one running around in a schoolgirl's gymslip.
Stevenson (*urgently*) Look outside and see if the coast is clear.

Mildred looks out of the door L

Holmes enters the top part of the lighthouse. He looks around, under the blankets and bed etc. He finds the flagon of wine and takes a sip. He registers approval as he sits on the bed

Mildred Nobody about. I think they're all down at the jetty.
Stevenson Right. I'm off. Now remember what I told you.
Mildred You are Alfred Fogerty and you're younger than I think because you've taken something.
Stevenson Very good.
Mildred It won't work.
Stevenson It will.

Stevenson exits L

Holmes sips from the flagon and looks at the books

Gloria enters R. *She has a towel around her*

Gloria Mrs Fogerty, there you are.
Mildred If you want shampoo you can't have any. There's a war on, you know.

Gloria No, I've taken my bath.
Mildred And you can't have toothpaste, either. I've only got denture powder.
Gloria I'd like my clothes, please.
Mildred I should think so. You can't go around like that.
Gloria Well?
Mildred Well what?
Gloria Where are they?
Mildred What?
Gloria My clothes.
Mildred How should I know?
Gloria I left them with you.
Mildred I've got more things to worry about than a forward young miss who can't keep her clothes on.

Mildred exits R

Gloria, bemused, sits on the crate UL

In the top part of the lighthouse Stevenson pokes his head up at the window, sees Holmes and ducks out of sight

Tomkins enters L

Tomkins (*looking around*) Gloria. Are you alone?
Gloria You could say that.
Tomkins Where's that good-for-nothing constable?
Gloria I've no idea.
Tomkins I sent him here to keep an eye on things. He needs a good dose of the army.
Gloria I've got another detecting job for you.
Tomkins (*unheeding*) My son Ronald's out there in North Africa, risking his life for his country and young pipsqueaks like Holmes get out of it.
Gloria I've lost my clothes.
Tomkins It isn't fair. He should be doing his bit like Ronald.
Gloria Are you going to find them for me?

Tomkins opens the upstage door

Tomkins (*yelling*) Holmes! Are you there?

Holmes listens, puts down the flagon and stands up

(*Going to Gloria*) Why, Gloria, where are your clothes?
Gloria I thought you'd never ask.
Tomkins (*suddenly amorous*) Oh, Gloria, Gloria. (*He sits beside her*)

Holmes exits from the top part of the lighthouse

Gloria (*wearily*) Walter, you're getting that look in your eye.
Tomkins (*putting his arms around her*) Oh, Gloria. Seeing you so much for the past two years has driven me insane.
Gloria It hasn't done me much good, either.

Tomkins I've devoted myself to righting the wrong that was done to you. Surely that deserves some recognition.

Gloria Won't you get a promotion?

Tomkins That means nothing. But just to hear you say you'll let me . . . let me . . .

Gloria (*struggling*) Let me go.

Tomkins pushes her back on crate and tries to kiss her

> *Holmes enters upstage. He is slightly drunk and watches Tomkins and Gloria, who do not see him*

Tomkins Surely you don't find me repulsive?

Gloria Why, Walter, why should I?

Holmes (*smiling drunkenly*) Because he is.

Tomkins and Gloria break in disarray

Tomkins (*mustering authority*) Holmes. About time.

Holmes (*right up to Tomkins; in his face*) You are repulsive. Repulsive . . . repulsive.

Tomkins (*aghast*) Constable!

Holmes Sergeant.

Gloria (*concerned*) John, I think you'd better——

Holmes (*to Tomkins*) And your old woman's repulsive, too.

Gloria I'm going to look for my clothes.

Gloria beats a hasty retreat R

Tomkins (*to Holmes*) This is one insubordination too many, Holmes.

Holmes And your bloody poodle's repulsive, too.

Tomkins That's enough.

Holmes And as for dear little Ronald, he's the most repulsive of all. Repulsive, repulsive, repulsive.

Tomkins My report on you, Constable——

Holmes Won't be anything near as lurid as my report on you, Sergeant.

Tomkins Holmes, I think——

Holmes (*taking out his notebook and pencil; pretending to write*) I did proceed into room whereupon I witnessed a person known to me as Sergeant Walter Ambrose Tomkins behaving in an unseemly manner with a female known to me as Gloria Fireknickers Lane. The subject forced his unwanted attentions on the aggrieved personage of Miss Lane taking advantage of her state of undress at the time. The subject said to the victim, "Oh, Miss Lane, I have longed for this moment."

Tomkins (*seething*) I did not.

Holmes You did. (*Pretending to write*) And then he proceeded to manipulate certain private areas of the aggrieved person's anatomy.

Tomkins Lies. All lies.

Holmes (*pretending to write*) I felt it my sworn duty to enquire of the subject what he thought he was doing. He replied, "Knickers to you, I'm out for a good time."

Tomkins Constable——
Holmes Sergeant.
Tomkins All right, Sergeant. I'll overlook this little outburst of yours.
Holmes Gee, Sergeant Tomkins, you're all heart.
Tomkins But just this once. And I might think twice about giving you a bad
report.
Holmes (*pretending to write*) The subject then tried to bribe the apprehend-
ing officer by saying——

Tomkins grabs the notebook from Holmes. He puts it in Holmes' pocket

Tomkins Don't overdo it, Sergeant.
Holmes (*smiling*) I won't—Sergeant.
Tomkins We can all make mistakes.
Holmes You know something? You *are* repulsive.

Adele enters R. *She wears Stevenson's clothes*

Adele Well, if it isn't the upholders of law and order. What's going on?
Tomkins Well, Mrs Delgrado has taken her daughter to their boat to get
some clothes for her to wear.
Adele And the Frenchman?
Tomkins He's around somewhere.
Holmes I don't trust him.
Adele Quite right. I don't think you should.
Tomkins (*perturbed*) Now look, Sergeant. Don't antagonize him.
Holmes Why? Because he's a big shot at the consulate?
Tomkins Well, we don't want to offend our allies, do we?
Holmes (*sarcastically*) We might get a bad report, mightn't we?
Tomkins I'm just saying that we'd better tread carefully.
Holmes (*smiling*) He's certainly got you scared.
Tomkins (*affronted*) Nonsense.
Adele (*moving to the door* L) Well, I'll just keep an eye on him.
Tomkins Just a moment, young lady.
Adele You mean you can tell I'm a lady in this outfit?
Tomkins There are some questions I'd like answered.
Adele Can't they keep?
Tomkins I'm afraid this is all a bit too much for me.
Holmes As the actress said to the bishop.
Tomkins (*laughing weakly*) Yes. Very funny, Holmes.
Adele OK, shoot.
Tomkins I'm interested to know why you were tied up a short while ago.
Adele Quite simple. I'm into bondage.
Tomkins Bondage?
Adele Yeah. How do you get *your* kicks?
Holmes He's into everything.
Tomkins (*to Adele*) You expect us to believe you tied yourself up?
Adele (*flippantly*) Yeah.
Tomkins With your hands behind your back?
Adele Sure.

Tomkins And gagged yourself?

Adele Why not?

Tomkins Miss Dumbrovski, I think I ought to tell you I am a detective sergeant and I am totally unconvinced of your story.

Adele Please yourself. (*She goes to the door* R)

Tomkins Where're you going?

Adele To take in the cool, salty air.

Tomkins I haven't finished with you.

Holmes I think she's finished with you. (*To Adele with a charming smile*) Miss Dumbrovski.

Adele Mrs.

Holmes Mrs Dumbrovski. Earlier you called Pierre by another name.

Adele (*innocently*) Did I?

Holmes Yes. You called him Maurice. Maurice Latoule.

Adele Oh yeah. Maurice Latoule was an old childhood sweetheart of mine. He gave me his pin. I always get mixed up with Frenchmen.

Holmes How do you know Pierre Dubois?

Adele I've never met him before.

Holmes Are you sure?

Adele Are you calling me a liar?

Holmes You said all hell's going to be let loose.

Adele Did I?

Holmes Yes. You said it twice.

Adele Schwineflugger's disease.

Holmes Pardon?

Adele Schwineflugger's disease. I suffer from it, you know.

Holmes No, I didn't know.

Adele Well, there you are.

Adele exits R

Tomkins I think you handled that most astutely, Sergeant Holmes.

Holmes Thank you, Sergeant Tomkins.

Tomkins Would you agree with me when I say that all we have to do now is find Alfred Fogerty?

Holmes I'd agree with that clever deduction.

Tomkins Then where the hell is he?

Holmes (*pointing to the upstage door*) Well, he's not up there. I've just looked.

Tomkins (*warmly*) Very good detective work, Sergeant.

Holmes (*modestly*) Mere formality.

Tomkins Why don't we search this island?

Holmes Good idea.

Tomkins There must be hundreds of places he could hide.

Holmes Just what I was thinking.

Tomkins You know, Sergeant, my report could lead to you getting a promotion.

Holmes That would be nice, if I wanted it.

Tomkins (*amazed*) You don't want promotion?

Holmes I've always wanted to be away from it all. This island would suit me fine.

Tomkins But don't you want more money?

Holmes Robinson Crusoe didn't have any.

Tomkins But he didn't have superannuation, either.

Holmes True. But staying here would suit me fine.

Tomkins And give up your career?

Holmes I wouldn't be giving up much. Shall we search for Fogerty?

Tomkins A good idea, Sergeant Holmes.

Tomkins and Holmes exit L

In the top part of the lighthouse Stevenson peeks through the window, sees no-one there and climbs in. He puts the bundle of clothes on the bed. He takes off the schoolgirl's uniform and throws it on floor. He picks up the clothing from the bed, only to discover as he puts it on that they are Gloria's clothes

Stevenson Oh no. I don't believe it. I just don't believe it. (*He sits dejectedly on the bed*)

Pierre enters L

Pierre Is anyone here? (*He sees that the upstage door is open and goes towards it*)

Mildred enters R

Mildred Where are you going?

Pierre I just wish to pay my compliments to Alfred.

Mildred He's not very well.

Pierre Then I will give him my condolences.

Mildred He's changed.

Pierre Into what? A carrot?

Mildred He's not what he was.

Pierre From what I have heard that would be an improvement.

Mildred He's got an exeter.

Pierre A what?

Mildred Something to make him younger.

Pierre Oh? An elixir? Very good.

Mildred Yes. He looks much younger than he really is.

Pierre (*humouring her*) That's fine.

Mildred He's really sixty-four.

Pierre Is that so?

Mildred Yes. But he looks twenty-four.

Pierre That is wonderful for you.

Mildred He made it himself.

Pierre What?

Mildred The exeter.

Pierre Really? He must be a very clever man.

Mildred Not really.

Pierre Is it all right for me to see him?

Mildred If you feel you have to.

Pierre exits upstage

(*To herself*) I don't know why Alfie's so popular all of a sudden. All through his life people kept avoiding him. Nobody liked him. Everybody used to look in the opposite direction when he came along. Now, suddenly everybody wants to know Alfred Fogerty. Everybody wants to meet him. Shake his hand. Talk to him. I can't think why. Once an obnoxious old coot always an obnoxious old coot I always say. (*Shrugging*) Oh well, maybe he had depths I never found. And never will.

She exits R

In the top part of the lighthouse Stevenson continues to sit on the bed

Pierre (*off*) Are you there, Mr Fogerty?

Stevenson dives under the blanket and covers his face

(*Off*) Mr Fogerty. Alfred.

Pierre enters the top part of the lighthouse. He sees Stevenson's form under the blanket

No need to be afraid of me, Alfred old chum. I am your contact.

Stevenson's arm comes out from under blanket. Pierre shakes hands

I am with the URGE. The Universal Reunification of the German Empire. I am Maurice Latoule.

Stevenson grunts

You and I have a destiny to keep. As you know, you have been planted here by the Axis for a certain occasion. Well, my friend, that occasion has arrived. In a very short time an Allied convoy will be approaching this very shore. They will depend on this lighthouse to guide them. Your orders are to dismantle this lighthouse; to render it inoperable. In short, you are to have a black-out.

Stevenson grunts from under the blanket

Mr Fogerty. Are you all right?

Stevenson grunts in the affirmative

You do understand the order?

Stevenson grunts

URGE is depending on you. Is there anything you wish to know?

Stevenson's head appears above the blanket

Stevenson Can you translate French into English?
Pierre (*shocked*) Mon Dieu! I don't believe it.
Stevenson What?

Pierre You look so ... so ...
Stevenson Young?
Pierre About twenty-one.
Stevenson Twenty-four, actually.
Pierre Pardon?
Stevenson I mean, I feel twenty-four. I'm really sixty-four.
Pierre I can't believe this.
Stevenson Didn't my wife tell you about my great discovery?
Pierre Yes. But ...
Stevenson It's great stuff.
Pierre Incredible.
Stevenson Yes, it is isn't it?
Pierre (*suspiciously*) What is your codename?
Stevenson That's easy. Mustardseed.
Pierre (*slightly impressed*) And your codenumber?
Stevenson Even easier. Two-nine-one-o-six-seven. You don't doubt I'm
    your man, do you?
Pierre No ... no. It is just that ...
Stevenson Relax, Maurice. Shall I tell you what I know about you?
Pierre You know about me?
Stevenson I'm in constant touch with URGE.
Pierre You are?
Stevenson Yes. You came here with a certain Daphne Delgrado, right?
Pierre Right.
Stevenson She's my daughter, right?
Pierre I suppose ...
Stevenson You cultivated her friendship in order to have a link with Alfred
    Fog—— I mean me. Right?
Pierre Right.
Stevenson And when she wanted to bring her daughter to this island that
    was your opportunity to contact me. Right?
Pierre Right.
Stevenson But there's a certain Yankee intelligence agent who's on to you.
    Right?
Pierre Ah yes. But what is his name?
Stevenson It's a her. And her name is Adele Dumbrovski. Right?
Pierre You are extremely well informed.
Stevenson (*crossing his fingers*) Me and URGE are just like that.
Pierre (*impressed*) Amazing. Truly amazing.
Stevenson (*modestly*) Oh it's nothing. I'm just a very important traitor.
Pierre No, I mean your youthful looks.
Stevenson (*flattered*) You really think I look twenty-one?
Pierre I would very much like to try this elixir of yours.
Stevenson All in good time, monsieur. First, you've got to do something for
    me.
Pierre But the convoy——
Stevenson It can wait. I want you to translate some naughty French books
    for me.

Pierre Perhaps some other time.
Stevenson Now. I've waited long enough.

Stevenson jumps out of bed and picks up a book. He sees Pierre staring at him in Gloria's clothes

Er, a side effect of the elixir.

Pierre Pardon?
Stevenson It, er, does something to the hormones.
Pierre (*feigning comprehension*) Oh. I see.
Stevenson (*showing a book to Pierre*) Now. Here. Tell me what that says.
Pierre (*reading*) It says "Allumettes à la Perigourdine".
Stevenson I know that. What is it in English?
Pierre Strips of puff pastry coated with puree of chicken livers.
Stevenson (*taken aback*) Is that all?
Pierre By no means.
Stevenson (*hopefully*) What else?
Pierre You must bake them in a moderate oven with finely chopped truffles.
Stevenson A moderate oven?
Pierre Personally, I prefer them slightly underdone.
Stevenson (*showing Pierre another book*) What about this one? What's that say?
Pierre In English?
Stevenson In English.
Pierre (*reading*) "First prepare your baking tray . . ."
Stevenson (*showing another book*) And this?
Pierre (*reading*) "Beat two eggs in a bowl and add garlic. Then toss the salad into a——"
Stevenson (*angrily*) All right. All right. A bloody cook book. All bloody cook books.
Pierre (*enthusiastically*) If you wish to learn how to do French cooking I can be of great assistance. My old aunt Brigette gave me some recipes that are magnifique. Do you like Consommé Brunoise?
Stevenson (*his anger building*) Get out of here, you French frog.
Pierre I have a superb recipe for Carrottes à la Vichy. You take half a kilo of carrots and you put them——
Stevenson Out!
Pierre But, monsieur——
Stevenson Out! Out! Out!

Stevenson kicks Pierre through the doorway

Pierre exits

In the main area of the lighthouse Daphne and Monica enter L. *Monica wears a child's party dress. She has sobered up slightly. Mildred enters* R

Mildred (*singing*) "Love is where you find it, tra la la la . . ." hello, dear.
Daphne Mother, I can't get any sense out of Monica.

Monica I haven't had any sense out of you for years.
Daphne (*appalled*) Monica. That's enough of that.
Mildred How can I help?
Daphne Where's Pierre?

*Pierre tumbles into the room through the upstage door. He picks himself up
self-consciously and trys to assume a superior air*

Pierre (*dusting himself off*) That will teach him a lesson he will not forget.
Daphne You've seen Father?
Pierre Yes.
Monica I want to see Grandad.
Pierre He is not in a hospitable mood right now.
Monica I bet he'd like to see me.
Daphne (*to Pierre*) I hope you didn't fight with him.
Pierre Our discussion was purely gastronomic.

Tomkins and Holmes enter L

Tomkins Ah, Mrs Fogerty. Just the person I wanted to see.
Mildred I thought you'd gone home.
Tomkins All in good time, Mrs Fogerty. All in good time.
Monica (*smiling at Holmes*) Hello.
Holmes (*smiling back*) Hello.
Tomkins (*to Mildred*) Where is Miss Lane?
Mildred Your girlfriend?
Tomkins (*embarrassed*) She is the chief witness in the case.
Daphne What case?
Holmes That's a good question.

Gloria enters R, still dressed in a towel

Gloria Did I hear my name mentioned?
Pierre Gloria. You look superb.
Holmes (*jealously*) Hey, watch it, froggy.
Gloria (*making eyes at Pierre*) Frenchmen do something to me.
Daphne Hey, watch it, Jezebel.
Gloria (*agressively*) You talking to me, fudge-face?
Daphne (*equally aggressively*) Well, I'm not talking to Winnie the Pooh,
    natty-knickers.
Gloria You looking for a fight?
Daphne You want one?
Monica Go on, Mum. Give it to her.
Pierre Please, please ladies. Do not fight over me.
Holmes You make me sick.
Tomkins Will everyone please calm down.
Pierre (*pointing at Holmes*) He started it.
Holmes I did not.
Daphne (*pointing at Gloria*) She started it.
Gloria I did not.
Monica (*to Tomkins*) You started it.

Tomkins Will everyone please calm down. Mrs Fogerty.
Mildred What?
Tomkins We want to see your husband.
Mildred I think I smell my carrot cake burning.

  Mildred exits hurriedly R

Tomkins Mrs Delgrado. We want to see your father.
Daphne I think I'd better give Mother a hand.

  Daphne exits R

Tomkins Monica. We want to see your grandfather.
Monica Mum might need some help.

  Monica exits R

Holmes (*to Tomkins*) Do you get the impression Alfred Fogerty doesn't exist?
Gloria Are you saying he's a pigment of my imagination?
Holmes I'm saying I couldn't care less.
Tomkins (*exasperatedly*) This has gone far enough.
Holmes As the actress said to the bishop.
Tomkins (*sitting on a crate*) I've had as much as I can take.

Tomkins looks hard at Holmes defying him to make his comment. Holmes grins back at him

Gloria Well, you're not going to get any sense out of this lot.
Tomkins Perhaps if we separate them ...
Holmes I'll go and get a crowbar.
Tomkins We might get some sense out of them one at a time.
Holmes (*to Gloria*) Isn't he a genius?
Gloria As usual, he's hit the nail right on the shaft.
Tomkins (*to Pierre*) We may as well start with you, Mr Dubois.
Pierre I can tell you nothing.
Tomkins We'll see. How long have you known Alfred Fogerty's daughter?
Pierre Oh, about five feet six inches.
Holmes (*unamused*) That's known as a Gallic joke.
Gloria And it got the Anglo-Saxon silence.
Tomkins (*to Pierre*) Well, monsieur?
Pierre I've known her about three weeks.
Tomkins Have you ever met Alfred Fogerty?
Pierre No.
Tomkins Then you don't know his whereabouts?
Pierre Yes.
Tomkins You do?
Pierre I meant—yes, I don't know his whereabouts.
Holmes You sure?
Pierre Why should I lie?
Tomkins Very well, that will be all.
Pierre You wish me to leave?

Tomkins If you would be so kind, monsieur.
Holmes Crawler.

Pierre goes to the door L

Gloria (*going to Pierre*) Hang on, Pierre. I'll go for a walk with you. I noticed a lovely little pathway leading down to a lovely little cove. We can explore together.
Holmes (*perturbed*) Hey, you can't go with him.
Gloria Why not?
Holmes Because ... because you're needed here. As a material witness.
Gloria Oh, go and fly a kite.

Gloria exits with Pierre

Holmes (*going to the door; calling*) You haven't any clothes on.
Tomkins Let her go, Sergeant.
Holmes But she has to identify Fogerty.
Tomkins We haven't found him yet.
Holmes I know but——
Tomkins Send someone else in.
Holmes Who?
Tomkins Oh, I don't know. Anybody.
Holmes Supposing they don't want to come in?
Tomkins (*amazed*) Good grief, man, we are upholders of the law. Make them come in. Use your authority.
Holmes I'm too nice for this job.

Holmes exits R

In the top part of the lighthouse Stevenson, wearing Gloria's clothes, climbs out of the window

Monica enters R *with Holmes*

Monica What do you want?
Holmes We just want to know if——
Tomkins Thank you. Sergeant. I'll ask the questions.
Holmes You ask your questions and I'll ask mine. (*To Monica*) What are you doing after school on Thursday?
Monica (*laughing*) Cheeky. I don't go to school. And I'm staying here.
Holmes Not much to do here.
Monica Oh, I don't know. What's your name?
Holmes John Holmes.
Monica Are you as well endowed as your namesake?
Holmes There's another John Holmes?
Monica No, I mean Sherlock.
Holmes Oh, him.
Monica Are you as clever as him?
Holmes Well, I remember a case I was on once which required a——
Tomkins Have you quite finished?
Holmes Quite.

Tomkins Why don't you have a look around?
Holmes I think I'm more use here.
Tomkins All right, but keep quiet. And take notes. Now, er ... Monica, isn't it?
Monica Monica Thérèse Angelina Maria Francesca May Delgrado.
Holmes (*writing*) May?
Monica That's spelt m-a-y.
Holmes (*wryly*) Thanks.
Monica You're welcome, John.
Tomkins When did you last see your grandfather?
Monica (*slightly unsurely*) Well, I ...
Tomkins Come on now. Did you see him when you went missing for that short time?
Monica Er, no.
Tomkins How did you lose your clothes, Monica?
Monica I don't know.
Tomkins Did you meet up with anyone else?
Monica (*uncertainly*) Well ...
Tomkins Yes?
Monica (*blurting*) Yes, I did see Grandad.
Tomkins Ha, ha. Where?
Monica At the top of the lighthouse.
Tomkins (*to Holmes*) You said there was nobody up there.
Holmes There isn't.
Tomkins Well, check again.
Holmes (*sending up Tomkins*) Check again, check again ...

Holmes exits upstage

Tomkins Now, Monica, you mustn't think of me as a big, bad ogre.
Monica What are you going to do to Grandad?
Tomkins We just want to see if he's all right.
Monica But if he's done nothing wrong, I mean, like dodging going in the army or something like that.
Tomkins He hasn't dodged the army.
Monica Then you won't take him away?

Holmes enters the top part of the lighthouse and searches around. He looks out of the window. He turns to see Monica's uniform and picks it up

Tomkins (*kindly*) I don't think so.
Monica Oh, that's good.
Tomkins You like your grandfather?
Monica Yes.

Holmes exits from the top part of the lighthouse, carrying the uniform

Tomkins Well, that will be all. Send your grandmother in, will you?
Monica When you find him will you tell him little Monica would like to play again?
Tomkins I'll tell him.

Monica And tell him I'll make him tingle again.

Tomkins is puzzled by this remark

Monica exits R

Holmes enters upstage

Holmes Sarge, look what I found.
Tomkins A school uniform?
Holmes It's Susan's.
Tomkins Susan?
Holmes Susan Hardcastle. She was wearing this only half an hour ago.
Tomkins Who the hell is Susan Hardcastle?
Holmes Annabelle's daughter.
Tomkins Who's Annabelle?
Holmes Mildred Fogerty's daughter.
Tomkins Her name's Daphne.
Holmes Her other daughter.
Tomkins Whose other daughter?
Holmes Mildred Fogerty.
Tomkins How come *I've* not met this Susan Hardcastle?
Holmes You were probably doing some heavy breathing with Miss Lane.
Tomkins Why didn't you tell me about her?
Holmes Oh, it's not important. The point is, she's getting around naked.
Tomkins (*a dreadful thought dawning*) My God, Holmes. She's been up there with . . . with him.
Holmes Yes.
Tomkins Without her clothes.
Holmes Right.
Tomkins And Monica's been up there too.
Holmes Without her clothes.
Tomkins (*remembering*) "Tell him I'll make him tingle again."
Holmes What?
Tomkins That's what Monica said.
Holmes Oh no. And don't forget what he did to Gloria.
Tomkins (*outraged*) Holmes, this man is a fiend incarnate. He must be found.
Holmes And then doctored.
Tomkins But how did he get up and down the tower without us knowing?
Holmes I noticed a lightning conductor outside the window. He must use that.
Tomkins He must be very agile for a sixty-four year old man.
Holmes (*looking at Monica's uniform*) I'd say he's *very* agile.

Mildred enters R

Mildred (*singing*) "Love is where you find it, tra la la la . . ." (*To Tomkins*) I hope this won't take long. I've got a carrot cake on the go.
Tomkins (*forgetting himself*) Stuff your carrot cake.
Mildred No need to be crude.

Tomkins Mrs Fogerty, I must insist on you telling me where your husband is.

Mildred He's gone fishing.

Tomkins Don't lie. He's been seen.

Holmes He lives at the top of the lighthouse, doesn't he?

Mildred (*wavering*) No ...

Holmes He has a bed up there and books and booze.

Mildred All right, all right. But he's done nothing wrong.

Tomkins Nothing wrong? Do you realize that at this very moment he is having his way with his own granddaughter?

Holmes There's a law against that.

Mildred But she's in there.

Tomkins Not Monica. Susan.

Mildred (*puzzled*) Susan?

Adele bursts in R

Adele Anybody got binoculars?

Tomkins Why?

Adele Because there's a convoy of ships due any minute and I want to see them.

Tomkins Haven't you seen ships before?

Adele Will you cut out the cackle and let me have some binoculars?

Tomkins I'd like to ask you some questions.

Adele Haysus Christus! You Limey cops never let up, do you?

Mildred I'll get you some binoculars. (*She goes to the door* R)

Tomkins I'd prefer you to stay here.

Mildred pays no attention. She exits R

I said I'd prefer——

Tomkins huffily exits R, *following Mildred*

Holmes (*smiling at Adele*) I love your outfit.

Adele Yeah. Real crazy.

Holmes I think I preferred you in your swimsuit, though.

Adele Yeah? Well, don't hold your breath until you see me in it again, bright eyes.

Tomkins enters R

Tomkins Holmes. Come in here and bring your notebook with you.

Tomkins exits R. *Holmes flashes Adele a big smile and exits* R

Adele sighs deeply. She turns on the radio but there is no response. She tries the upstage door, finds it open and exits

Stevenson enters the main area L. *He peers cautiously around before venturing in*

Stevenson (*half whispering*) Mildred. Mildred.

The door R *opens. Stevenson ducks out of sight behind a crate*

Monica enters R *and crosses to the door* L

Stevenson sees her

Monica.

Monica There you are. I was just going to climb up and see you. I see you found your clothes.

Stevenson These aren't mine. Look, will you do me a favour?

Adele enters the top part of the lighthouse and looks around

Adele Mr Fogerty?

Monica (*to Stevenson*) What do you want me to do?

Stevenson Get my clothes from Mildred and bring them up to the tower for me.

Adele Mr Fogerty, I must see you.

Monica All right.

Stevenson And there's no need to climb up the lightning conductor. You can go up the stairs.

Adele looks under the bed, finds the flagon and takes a sip

Monica What about the clothes you're wearing?

Stevenson takes off Gloria's clothes and puts them on the crate

Stevenson Here, you take them. Give them back to whoever they belong to.

Monica (*taking the clothes*) See you soon.

Stevenson Yes. Don't be too long. I'll hang on to these for safe keeping.

Stevenson picks up Monica's school uniform and exits upstage

Daphne enters R

Daphne Monica. What are you up to? I've been worried about you.

Monica You don't have to worry about me, Mother dearest.

Daphne Have you seen Monsieur Dubois?

Monica No.

Daphne (*taking the clothes from Monica*) These belong to Miss Lane.

Monica I know. I'm trying to find her.

Daphne And I'm trying to find Pierre. And something tells me they may be together somewhere.

Daphne puts Gloria's clothes on the crate and strides purposefully out L, *followed by Monica*

Stevenson enters the top part of the lighthouse. He is startled to see Adele

Stevenson All right, mate. What's the big idea?

Adele Hi there.

Stevenson (*throwing Monica's uniform on the bed*) Who are you? Mildred's new boyfriend?

Adele I'm not a boy.

Stevenson Listen, mate, if you have any intentions of—hey, they're my clothes you're wearing.

Adele Listen, sunshine, forget that.
Stevenson Get them off.
Adele Will you listen to me?
Stevenson I want my clothes. (*He grabs hold of Adele*)

Adele struggles as he tries to take his clothes off her

   Monica's face appears at the window and she registers concern at what she sees

Stevenson and Adele fall on to the bed

Adele Will you cool it?
Stevenson (*taking Adele's trousers off; heatedly*) I want my clothes.

Adele puts a judo hold on Stevenson and renders him helpless on the bed

   Monica's face disappears from view

Adele Will you listen to me, you stupid son of an Indiana quack?
Stevenson I'm listening.
Adele You can have your goddam clothes. Personally, I wouldn't be caught dead in them.
Stevenson Then why wear them?
Adele Shut up and listen. There's a guy on this island calling himself Pierre Dubois.
Stevenson I know. I've met him.
Adele You have? (*She relaxes the judo hold*)
Stevenson Yes. He's trying to sabotage this lighthouse so that a big convoy will get wrecked.
Adele Very good.
Stevenson He thinks I'm Alfred Fogerty.
Adele And who are you really?
Stevenson Never mind.
Adele OK. It doesn't matter. Keep being Alfred Fogerty for a while.
Stevenson Why?
Adele I want you to help me get something from the slimy Frenchman.
Stevenson Compromising photos?
Adele You're not with Intelligence, are you?
Stevenson I keep my ears open.
Adele Smart boy.
Stevenson I've got my wits about me.
Adele Pity you couldn't hang on to your clothes, though.
Stevenson What do I do?
Adele Dubois will be seeing you again. He's got to. Now you get those photographs from him some way and then I'll take over. Meanwhile I'll wear this. (*She picks up Monica's uniform. She starts to unbutton her shirt, sees Stevenson looking intently at her, and stops*) I'll go out there.

   Adele leaves the top part of the lighthouse taking Monica's uniform

Stevenson puts on the trousers she has left behind

Holmes enters R. *He looks around*

Daphne enters L

Holmes Ah, Mrs Delgrado. I was just looking for you. The sarge wants to ask you some questions.
Daphne (*agitatedly*) I've lost her.
Holmes Who?
Daphne My little girl. I turned my back and there she was—not there.
Holmes (*reassuringly*) I wouldn't worry too much about her. I think she's capable of looking after herself.
Daphne I'm a caring mother.
Holmes And a wonderful job you do too.
Daphne Where's Pierre?
Holmes He went to look at a lovely cove.
Daphne With that Gloria woman I suppose?
Holmes Well . . . Yes, as a matter of fact.
Daphne I knew it. Men. They're all the same. Despicable.
Holmes I couldn't agree more.
Daphne Immoral beasts.
Holmes Brutes.
Daphne Swines.
Holmes Listen, if you take that pathway to the right you might come across them.
Daphne To the right?
Holmes Yes. I'll tell the sarge I couldn't find you.
Daphne Down by the cove?
Holmes Yes. Happy hunting.

Daphne exits L *and Holmes exits* R

Adele enters the top part of the lighthouse. She wears Monica's uniform. She throws Stevenson's clothes to him

Adele There's your precious clothes. Now listen, whoever you are. I'm trusting you.
Stevenson (*dressing*) I'm all for the cause.
Adele You just sit tight.
Stevenson That's easy.
Adele And keep Latoule away from the mechanism.
Stevenson I just want one favour from you.
Adele What's that?
Stevenson When you get back to the states will you get Ingrid Bergman's autograph for me?
Adele Sure.
Stevenson And Joan Crawford's?
Adele Yeah.
Stevenson And Betty Grable's?
Adele Yeah, yeah. I know them all personally. Right. I'm off.

Adele exits from the top part of the lighthouse

Tomkins and Holmes enter R

Tomkins Well, Holmes, what do you make of that?
Holmes Elementary, my dear Tomkins. Elementary.
Tomkins Do you believe her?
Holmes Yes.
Tomkins You really believe this Fogerty fellow has concocted a brew that makes him forty years younger?
Holmes Yes. I've tried it.
Tomkins You've tried it?
Holmes Yes. And it made me feel like a ten year old.
Tomkins You've actually drunk some?
Holmes Yes. It's under his bed.
Tomkins (*aggrieved*) Sergeant, I think you should share these discoveries with your partner.

Tomkins and Holmes sit on a crate

Adele enters upstage, sees them, and ducks back again

Holmes I didn't think you'd be interested, Sarge.
Tomkins It's all material evidence.
Holmes True.
Tomkins I wouldn't mind sampling this elixir. In the line of duty, of course.
Holmes Of course.
Tomkins (*thoughtfully*) Forty years younger, eh?
Holmes That's right.

Monica enters L

Tomkins Monica.
Monica (*tearfully*) I want my mum.
Tomkins Yes, of course. But first, I want to ask you about your grandfather.
Monica (*sobbing*) He's horrible.
Tomkins But you said you liked him.
Monica Not any more.
Tomkins Why?
Monica He's unfaithful.

Tomkins and Holmes exchange meaningful glances

Tomkins Oh?
Monica Yes. He was tearing her clothes off.

More meaningful glances

Tomkins No?
Monica Yes.
Holmes The bounder.
Monica Yes.
Tomkins Where is he now?
Monica Up at the top.

Tomkins Monica, how old does he look?
Monica A lot younger than you.
Holmes Would you say younger than me?
Monica Yes. I want my mum.

Monica exits R

Holmes Well, Sarge, it sounds like he's discovered the formula.
Tomkins Let's get a sample.

Tomkins and Holmes go to the upstage door

Adele enters before they reach it

Adele Well, well, if it isn't my two favourite sleuths.
Holmes It's Susan Hardcastle.
Adele Susan went home.
Tomkins Is Alfred Fogerty up there?
Adele Yes.
Tomkins How old does he look?
Adele Not as ancient as you, Grandpa.
Tomkins Then it's true.
Holmes That's where he gets his energy from.
Tomkins Come on, Holmes.
Adele Now just a minute——
Tomkins Later, Mrs Dumbrovski. Later.

Tomkins and Holmes exit upstage

Gloria dashes in L

Gloria Has Pierre come through here?
Adele No.
Gloria I'm worried.
Adele Why?
Gloria He's got an axe.
Adele Really?
Gloria Yes, from the tool shed. He's gone berserk.
Adele Don't worry. The police will take care of him.
Gloria (*picking up her clothes*) There they are.
Adele Look, why don't you tell me about it over a cup of tea?

Adele and Gloria exit R

Tomkins and Holmes enter the top part of the lighthouse

Tomkins All right, Fogerty. Police here.
Stevenson All right. It's a fair cop.
Tomkins Are you Alfred Fogerty?
Stevenson Yes.
Tomkins My God. It's true.
Holmes He *does* look younger than you.
Tomkins And you. (*To Stevenson*) Were you in Liverpool on the night of February the fourteenth, nineteen forty-two?

Stevenson Yes.

Tomkins I charge you with the attempted rape of Miss Gloria Lane in an air raid shelter——

Stevenson Hey, wait a minute. I didn't do that.

Tomkins That's for a jury to decide.

Stevenson I'm innocent.

Holmes I must warn you that anything you say——

Stevenson I don't know anything about attempted rape.

Holmes That's what they all say.

Stevenson Now just hang on there——

Tomkins Where's this elixir of yours?

Stevenson The what?

Holmes It's under the bed.

Tomkins brings the flagon out from under the bed

Tomkins So this is your little secret, eh?

Stevenson All right, so it's illegal. I didn't think——

Tomkins Didn't think we were on to you, eh? (*He takes a sip and then a big gulp from the flagon*)

Stevenson Er, you'd better take it easy.

Tomkins (*intensely*) Easy? Easy? Don't talk to me about easy. (*He takes a big gulp*) I want my youth back. My vitality. My power. (*He gulps*) Do you think it's easy to be me, eh? (*He gulps*) To be my age? To be what I am? I'm really young at heart, you know. (*He gulps*) Yes, I am. I'm young, I'm carefree, lively and gay. You can laugh, but I don't want to be me. (*He gulps*) I want to go back. Back to Felicity Martin. She was my one love. (*He gulps*) Oh Felicity, Felicity where are you? I love you. We were so happy together. (*He gulps*) Oh Felicity my love, my little tootsy-wootsy. Remember Walter? You used to call me your little aphrodisiac. (*He gulps*) Your little . . . your little . . . little . . . (*He falls back on the bed, asleep*)

Holmes (*taking out his notebook*) All right, what's your name?

Stevenson Alfred Fogerty.

Holmes Don't give me that. I don't fall for this youthful elixir flapdoodle.

Stevenson All right. My name's Malcolm Stevenson.

Holmes (*writing*) Is that Stevenson with a V or a PH?

Stevenson It's Stevenson with an S.

Holmes And why are you here?

Stevenson I might as well tell you. I'm hiding.

Holmes From what?

Stevenson The war.

Holmes I see.

Stevenson You can take me away. I won't resist.

Holmes Well, let's not be too hasty.

Stevenson (*picking up the flagon*) Drop of carrot wine?

Holmes I don't mind if I do.

Stevenson and Holmes pass the flagon backwards and forwards during the following conversation

Stevenson What sort of a sentence do you think I'll get?
Holmes For failure to register for military service?
Stevenson Yes.
Holmes Don't worry. Your secret is safe with me.
Stevenson You're true blue.
Holmes I know.
Stevenson I think war is stupid.
Holmes So do I.
Stevenson Who's winning, by the way?
Holmes The last I heard it was us twenty, them thirteen.
Stevenson Great.
Holmes Where's Fogerty?
Stevenson Fogerty?
Holmes Don't play dumb.
Stevenson Oh, Fogerty?
Holmes Right.
Stevenson He's dead.
Holmes Dead?
Stevenson That's right.
Holmes Foul play?
Stevenson Could be.
Holmes Look, Stevenson, I'm not going to give you away so let's be honest, eh?
Stevenson All right. Alfie's with the angels. Snuffed it. Gone for a burton. Cashed in his chips. He's playing a——
Holmes How?
Stevenson Well, you might as well know. I met him two years ago in Liverpool. He was on holiday. I was desperate to find somewhere safe to hide for the duration of the war.
Holmes And he brought you here?
Stevenson Yes. Then one night he and Mrs Fogerty had a fight.
Holmes What about?
Stevenson The quality of her carrot cakes.
Holmes I see.
Stevenson No you don't. You've never tasted her carrot cakes.
Holmes So where is he now?
Stevenson Buried under the carrot patch outside the front door. She hit him over the head with a shovel.
Holmes Poor old Alfie. All the time we've been looking for him he's been pushing up carrots.

Holmes and Stevenson continue to get inebriated

Pierre enters L. *He looks wild and carries an axe. He strides to the upstage door*

Mildred enters R. *She carries binoculars*

Mildred Oh, *excusez-moi*, silver plates——
Pierre Stay away from me.

Mildred What are you doing, Mr—— er . . . er . . .
Pierre (*looking heavenwards*) Merde.
Mildred What are you doing, Mister Merde?
Pierre Please excuse me.
Mildred Where are you going?
Pierre To see your husband.
Mildred With an axe?
Pierre Believe me, it is not for him.
Mildred Have you got an urge?
Pierre Oui.
Mildred Would you like a slice of carrot cake?
Pierre Later.

Pierre exits upstage

Mildred (*calling after him*) I'll be waiting for you, Mr Merde. Don't do too
much damage, will you? Please be careful how you swing that axe. (*To
herself*) I blame Baldwin. He's never lived in a lighthouse so he wouldn't
care. (*She fiddles with the radio. Nothing happens*) And I'm missing Victor
Sylvester.

Mildred exits R

*Pierre enters the top part of the lighthouse. Stevenson sees him and grabs
him. They struggle for possession of the axe*

Pierre Release me, you stupid old imbecile.
Stevenson Not likely.

*As they grapple Holmes hits Pierre on the head with an extra large cook book.
Pierre falls unconscious on the bed next to Tomkins*

Holmes That will teach the oversexed swine. (*He gulps from the flagon*)
Stevenson You have just saved western civilization as we know it.
Holmes Thanks. But I don't want to know it. (*He sinks slowly to the floor*)

Stevenson grabs the flagon from him and takes a gulp

Stevenson Do you think I'll get some kind of medal? A pension for life,
maybe? A peerage? Or a night out with Norma Shearer? (*He slowly sinks
to the floor*) An autographed photo of Shirley Temple? A lock of George
Raft's hair? A packet of Woodbines? (*He passes out*)

Mildred enters R. *She goes to the upstage door and listens. She closes the
door and locks it*

Mildred (*singing*) "Love is the sweetest thing, la da de da de . . ."

Daphne enters L *in angry mood*

Daphne I've had all I can take.
Mildred As the actress said to the bishop.
Daphne I'm not staying here another minute.
Mildred I think you're very wise.

Daphne If Pierre wants that cheap edition of Tallulah Bankhead he can have her.

Mildred Quite right.

Daphne I think Monica's safer on the mainland. Where is she?

Mildred (*pointing* R) In there.

Daphne The poor child has too many temptations here.

Daphne exits R

Mildred (*singing*) "Love makes the world go round, tra la tra la . . ."

Adele and Gloria enter R

Adele goes to the radio and switches it on .

You won't get anything.

Adele We'll see.

Mildred Here's the binoculars.

Adele (*fiddling with the radio*) I don't need them now.

Gloria Where are the brave boys in blue?

Mildred Haven't you heard?

Gloria Heard what?

Mildred They've gone.

Gloria Gone?

Adele Gone?

Mildred And they've taken Mister Merde with them.

Gloria The Frenchman?

Mildred Yes. It seems he had an urge to chop up the lighthouse.

Gloria But what about me?

Mildred No. I think he only wanted to chop up the lighthouse.

Gloria Oh. That's great, I must say.

Adele Shush, I'm getting something.

Radio Newscaster's Voice ". . . and Parliament agreed it should be all over by Christmas. The convoy from the USA which was re-routed via the Hebrides has arrived safely in Liverpool. It experienced no enemy attacks during the voyage which was described as uneventful. George Formby made a personal appearance today at an aircraft factory in Blackburn, Lancashire, where he played his banjo and . . ."

Adele switches off the radio

Mildred We're missing *Hi Gang*.

Adele Well, I'm off.

Gloria Me too. (*To Mildred*) Tell your husband I wanted to meet him again to give him these. (*She takes out a pair of braces from her pocket which she hands to Mildred*)

Mildred Alfie's braces.

Gloria And tell him, "Thanks for a lovely night".

Daphne enters with Monica

Daphne (*to Monica*) No need to carry on like that. I've made up my mind.

Monica But, Mum . . .
Daphne We are leaving.
Monica Without seeing Grandad?
Daphne He's gone fishing.
Adele Any chance of a lift?
Daphne You're welcome.
Gloria And me?
Daphne (*dubiously*) Well, I suppose it's all right.
Mildred Bon voyage, everybody.
Daphne Mother, why don't you and Father give up this life?
Mildred And come and live with you?
Daphne (*hastily*) On second thoughts, it does seem a nice, healthy place to live.
Mildred Mister Merde said everyone in France and Britain has been denuded.
Gloria Really?
Mildred Yes. Completely denuded. He says Churchill ordered it.
Adele (*to Mildred*) Are you sure he said denuded?
Mildred His very words.
Adele I knew times were bad, but——
Daphne (*impatiently*) Are you coming?

Daphne takes Monica's hand and moves to the door L

Adele I'm coming.
Gloria (*to Mildred*) Love to Alfie.
Monica Mum, do you know how useful a carrot can be?

Daphne and Monica exit L *followed by Adele and Gloria*

Mildred switches the radio on. She takes a key out of her pocket and opens the upstage door

Mildred exits, closing the door behind her

The radio plays a female vocal version of "I'm In The Mood For Love" as—

the CURTAIN *falls*

FURNITURE AND PROPERTY LIST

ACT I

On stage: Large crates with lids UR and UL
Tea-chests
Packing cases
Boxes. *On one:* radio
Strings, wires. *On them:* ships' lanterns, shells etc.

ON RAISED AREA UR
Camp bed. *On it:* blanket. *Under it:* large flagon of wine
Books scattered on floor

Off stage: 2 glasses of lemonade **(Mildred)**
Bundle of **Stevenson**'s clothes **(Mildred)**
Bundle of **Stevenson**'s clothing including a pair of underpants **(Mildred)**
Towel **(Adele)**
Basket of carrots **(Mildred)**

Personal: **Mildred:** key to upstage door, rag
Tomkins: gun
Holmes: bullet, notebook, pencil

ACT II

On stage: As Act I

Off stage: Bundle of **Stevenson**'s clothes **(Mildred)**
Stevenson's clothes **(Adele)**
Axe **(Pierre)**
Binoculars **(Mildred)**

Personal: **Pierre:** photographs
Mildred: 2 keys to upstage door
Holmes: notebook, pencil
Gloria: pair of braces

EFFECTS PLOT

Please read the notice concerning the use of copyright music and recordings on page iv.

ACT I

No cues

ACT II

Cue 1   **Adele:** "Shush, I'm getting something."   (Page 54)
Radio Newscaster as in text

Cue 2   **Mildred** *exits*   (Page 55)
Radio plays female vocal version of "I'm In The Mood For Love"

LIGHTING PLOT

Property fittings required: nil
A lighthouse interior. The same scene throughout

ACT I. Evening

To open: General interior lighting on main and raised areas

No cues

ACT II. Evening

To open: General interior lighting on main and raised areas

No cues

MADE AND PRINTED IN GREAT BRITAIN BY
LATIMER TREND & COMPANY LTD PLYMOUTH
MADE IN ENGLAND